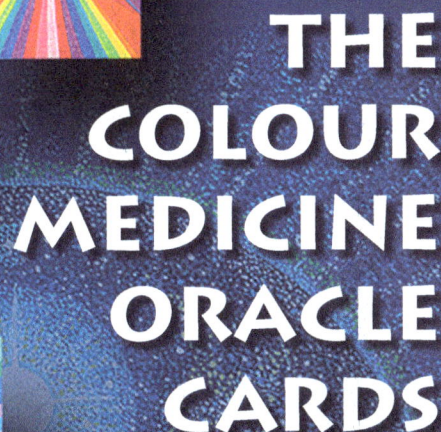

THE COLOUR MEDICINE ORACLE CARDS

THE LAWS OF LIGHT IN HEALING WITH COLOUR CODES

SYLVIA MEISSNER

First published 2021 by Sylvia Meissner

Text © Sylvia Meissner 2021
Design © Healing Art Design Pty Ltd 2021

All rights reserved – no part of this book may be reproduced or utilised in any form or by any means electronic or mechanical, including photocopying and recording or by any information storage and retrieval system without permission in writing from the Publisher.

The Colour Medicine Oracle Card Deck are registered trademarks.

Edited by Sylvia Meissner
Typeset by Post Pre-press Group, Brisbane

Paintings by Sylvia Meissner
https://www.healingartdesign.com.au/
facebook.com/Healing Art Design Pty Ltd

A catalogue record for this book is available from the National Library of Australia.

ISBN 978-0-6450006-3-4

Note to the Reader (Disclaimer):
This oracle card deck has been created for divination purposes only. Any information on colour therapy can be incorporated into a level of 'self help healing'.

The meditations and positive affirmations are tools to provide an understanding for self-empowerment.

These techniques and approaches described herein are for spiritual practices for enlightenment, unfoldment and awareness about colour consciousness for mankind. This information is not to be substituted for professional, medical care or treatment. They should not be used to treat a serious ailment without prior consultation with a qualified health care professional. Any use to which the recommendations, ideas and techniques are put is at the reader's sole discretion and risk.

< Previous page: Blue Meditation Banner by Sylvia Meissner designed by Art House Reproductions.

HEALING THROUGH COLOUR AND MOTHER NATURE!

Sylvia Meissner

CONTENTS

Introduction	1
Creating the Colour Medicine Cards	5
Introducing Colour Medicine for the 21st Century	8
The Spiritual Psyche of Colour for Mankind	12
Creating the Colour Geometry Chakra Maps	19
Colour Representation of Every Chakra	24
Abundance	29
Acceptance	31
Action	33
Angelic Guidance Geometry Map	35
Balance	37
Base Chakra Geometry Map	39
Belief	41
Bliss	43
Breakthrough	45
Celebration	47
Chakra Healing	49
Climate Review	51
Commitment	53
Compassion	55
Confusion	57
Creativity	61
Crown Chakra Geometry Map	63
Disillusion	65
Exploration	67
Fertility	69
Flexibility	71
Focus	73
Forgiveness	75
Freedom	77

Friendship	81
Harvest	83
Healing	85
Heart Chakra Geometry Map	87
Independence	89
Integrity	91
Karma	93
Light Child	95
Loss	97
Luck	99
Magic	101
Manifestation	103
Meditation	105
Movement	107
Nature	109
Navel Chakra Geometry Map	111
Negativity	113
New Beginnings	115
Obsession	117
Obstacle	119
Partnership	121
Patience	123
Persistence	125
Philosophy	127
Play	129
Power	131
Prayer	133
Protection	135
Psychic Growth	137
Purpose	139
Reflection	141
Relaxation	143
Romance	145
Sacred Site	147
Solar Plexus Geometry Map	149
Solitude	151
Soul Growth	153
Stagnation	155

Strength	157
Surrender	159
Third Eye Chakra Geometry Map	161
Throat Chakra Geometry Map	163
Time Travel	165
Transcendence	167
Transformation	169
Trust	171
Universe	173
Wholeness	175
Wisdom	177
Wishes	179
The Auric Colour Field of the Body Chakras	181
How Does Colour Healing Work?	184
Positive Affirmations for Healing	186
How to Use the Oracle Cards	187
How to Balance Chakras with its Opposite Colour	196
Meditation and Visualisation Techniques for Healing	197
Psychic Protection and Grounding Techniques	199
A Spiritual Message From the Artist	202
Biography of the Artist	205
Contact Details for Purchasing Art	210
Acknowledgements	214
Recommended Further Reading	216
More Information on the Artist and Order Details for Art and Giclee Reproduction Art Prints	217

INTRODUCTION

The Colour Medicine Oracle Cards introduces a new vision of colour therapy for the 21st century.

These self-help healing cards have been created and written by Sylvia Meissner, who works in the field as a healer, artist, colour therapist, psychic, tarot reader and spiritual counsellor.

The oracle deck has been designed to work with 'colour vibrational energy healing', which can be applied to the Chakras that are found within the bodies of mankind.

Colour has a powerful influence on mankind and if implemented properly can help to heal, bring in balance and harmonise the body Chakras in order to help to maintain good health and inner wellbeing.

The use of colour can also affect one's mood, mental state, emotional and spiritual being.

The oracle deck has been inspired by the artist and creator to offer 'healing through colour and nature!'

Her pioneering spirit and vision connects to the field of light sciences where colour and light energy will become the new founded medicine for the future generations to understand and to use.

The application for the use of colour explained by the artist has a purpose for mankind; to enlighten one's own senses.

The artist explores the spiritual code of colour represented by every single letter in the word as follows:

C for cosmos
O for omnipresent
L for light
O for Om
U for universe
R for ray

Colour has been around since the birth of the earth. The universe was created by light and energy from a divine power. Without colour, there would be no life!

By implementing a level of 'colour healing' into our own life, this energy derived from the cosmos certainly has a powerful influence for the mind, body and soul of every living being.

Colour therapy is the new vision for mankind living in the 21st century. Nature, that is filled with and explores colour, plays a vital role toward the constitution of mankind's health, balance and further evolution in life.

The oracle cards represent an assortment of colourful images of Mother Nature, stars of light, universal heavenly bodies, visionary art and complex geometry Chakra maps for healing.

These images have been designed and created by the artist.

The Colour Medicine Oracle Cards have been developed to help advance mankind's evolution. By understanding and learning the principles of 'light energy', it is possible to shift mankind's level of consciousness to a higher plane of awareness.

Mankind is a 'light being'. Everything in life is made up of energy and matter. The healing aspect of every oracle card connects to a field of light energy. We can absorb these colours through the eyes and our skin to bring in balance, energy and harmony for the body's Chakras.

Colour is a living energy and a language of its own.

The artist connects her level of creativity with nature. It is the beauty of the planet that inspires a translation of light and colour as a form of healing energy called 'chi'. These tiny power points of thousands of dots, a technique called 'Pointillism and Divisionism of Colour', has been applied to every artwork image.

The human body requires the full spectrum of colour and light for survival, health, direction, balance, wholeness, motivation and for peace of mind.

Every artwork image of the oracle card deck has a level of 'chi energy' where the flow of the colour field helps to open, activate for balance and to re-energise the Chakras. A person may become magnetised or attuned to a particular art work that incorporates a flow of colours for healing, upliftment, calmness, revitalisation, peace, inspiration etc.

One's thoughts, values and attributes are held within the Chakras, which are brought forward to our conscious mind through to the physical brain. When the Chakras change, our thought patterns will also change.

The human mind is a powerful organ that controls and regulates our body's health system. The way we are conditioned to think, our emotions, spiritual outlook in life and our external environment all has an influence on who we are.

If a person feels sad, depressed or has a negative thought outlook in life, these unfavourable psychological conditions can affect the energy flow of the body to become sluggish and 'out of balance'. This reaction over time can create some form of illness or dis-easement in the body. A transformative process is required to confront any damaging psychological issues to bring in healing and wholeness for the body.

Unite the inner spirit, soul, and physical being for wellness!

Other chapters in the book further explore and explain the concept of colour therapy.

Every oracle card connects to a message that can be used as a 'divination tool' to help direct one's life.

The oracle card deck taps into the spiritual laws of life, which further offers wisdom, guidance and positive affirmations to use and also informs the reader alongside meditation techniques for healing through colour.

It is a complex package of spiritual knowledge that has been simplified to make it easy to understand and to use.

The oracle cards further explain the natural workings of 'universal law', which include how to attract abundance, wellbeing and positive growth.

Nature and earth are all connected as one. These cards inform the reader of a spiritual message concerning planetary and environmental awareness.

The artist and creator of the oracle deck has in previous art exhibitions held overseas in Hong Kong, Dubai, Shanghai and New York, promoted the concepts of 'The Fragility of Nature', 'Global Warming' and 'Colour Medicine for the 21st Century'. Through these art exhibitions the works express a message to preserve and conserve nature, to protect endangered species on earth and the healing aspects of colour for mankind.

Mankind has to learn to work in harmony with Mother Nature and to share the earth with all other living creatures. All nations of the world are experiencing global climatic change due to the earth and Mother Nature being out of balance!

Mother Nature, which is a supernatural power of its own, is trying to restore the earth's balance by taking action. Mother Nature controls the weather patterns around the globe. The earth is a living energy network that needs to be nurtured, not to be polluted and destroyed. Mankind has to take responsibility to look after the welfare of our precious planet.

Mankind has a challenge to further develop the spiritual plane within them known as 'the sixth sense', which connects to the world of light and spirit. The creation of the Colour Medicine Oracle Cards will help to achieve this level of spiritual unfoldment and enlightenment for mankind. Hopefully at the same time, mankind will try to accomplish balance for the planet to make it a better world to live in.

The Rainbow Cosmic Sun Light Ray Painting by Sylvia Meissner.

CHAPTER ONE

CREATING THE COLOUR MEDICINE CARDS

The concept for the oracle deck began in the year of 2007.

The idea germinated from the artist and with the help of her spirit friends from the other side. A new spiritual guardian was introduced whilst writing the book. The artist was kindly greeted by a spirit being from another time and space dimension called Tao. The process of receiving information from another source is called 'channelling'. This automatic process is where one opens up to connect to a guide, a person or an unknown energy that exists in another time zone that is not perceived on the earth plane but can be found in the veil of spirit. By placing a pen to paper and allowing it to happen without interference from your own mind, this form of writing became spontaneous. These channellings from Tao represent his role as the 'guardian' of the earth star.

The word Tao means 'to analyse oneself – in order to assist our world'. The channellings delivered by Tao means to unify all forces of nature, the supernatural and other time zones found within the universe for harmony and balance.

The mission of working with Tao is to help heal the earth and to raise the level of consciousness of mankind, offering spiritual unfoldment and enlightenment. The information from Tao, who is also a 'star gazer', has the ability to predict unforeseen events involving Mother Earth's destiny. The message from Tao explains that the role for mankind being on the earth is to become the 'greenkeeper' as a life role to honour, respect and to take responsibility for the welfare of the planet. Mankind has been given an intellect and a heart to know what is right.

The actions of mankind that pollute, destroy and disrupt the natural ecology of the land, sea and air have serious implications that affect the food chain of all of life. All other living species are dependent on this food chain. If this food chain changes, it can create a negative impact on the environment that includes a loss of natural inhabitants and habitats.

The earth is experiencing global climatic change, where Mother Nature is trying to restore the balance within the natural ecosystem. Mother Nature is warning us that the earth is out of balance! Mankind must learn to perceive from a higher plane of awareness in order to take some form of positive action to save the planet.

By combining the artist's and Tao's work as one, these oracle cards have been created to help advance mankind's evolution through spiritual awareness. These oracle deck cards do have a mission and a purpose to also introduce the light energy of colour healing to the 21st century.

The oracle deck brings together spiritual concepts of healing through colour therapy, displays a Chakra colour code bar system on every oracle card, contains eight powerful geometry Chakra maps that can be used as visualisation tools to correct energy flow for every Chakra, offers positive affirmations to use, meditation techniques for the Chakras, universal knowledge for guidance and beautiful artwork images of Mother Nature for inspiration. The oracle deck has been created for every individual to use, to help give guidance and a form of 'self-help healing'.

The principles of colour light therapy included in the oracle deck for healing, helps to bring in balance and harmony for the Chakras that are found within the bodies of mankind. The futuristic vision for mankind in the realm of healing introduces colour medicine for the 21st century. Light technology for healing will continue to grow, becoming the 'New Age science of medicine'.

The practical application of light energy into the future will be used to heal any form of dis-easement through vibration, sound and colour rays. The futuristic vision for using colour therapy implies that operations or surgeries that pierce the body of mankind will not be necessary. Most treatments will use light energy for healing.

The artist connects to colour as a source of energy for healing. Over the years working in her own holistic practice as a healer and a spiritual guidance counsellor, her clients have been invaluable and inspirational exploring all depths of life's problems. The content of the oracle book relates to these subject matters, which is self-explanatory in offering wisdom and guidance.

Anyone working in the field of holistic therapy certainly has a responsibility in helping others. She sees herself as a 'soul mechanic' where she is able to tune into the human psyche, which explores the emotional, mental, spiritual and physical aspects of the body.

As the creator of the Colour Medicine Oracle Cards, her other passion and study of works have included esoteric knowledge, palmistry, numerology, theosophy, philosophy, Buddhism, reiki, crystal healing, colour therapy, metaphysics and understanding the laws of spirit. These spiritual concepts have influenced the 'bulk body' of information for guidance, healing and wisdom into the oracle deck.

The oracle deck explores the spiritual pathway for every soul that has entered the earth plane, to work through dharma and other life lessons for soul growth. Mankind living in the 21st century is approaching a level of rapid ascension for spiritual growth to assist working from another plane of higher consciousness.

The oracle cards intend to help facilitate this process of higher learning. By gaining universal knowledge every human being can begin to heal the world with peace and joy. This is a way of finding forgiveness and to end the suffering that people must endure during war or any other conflict, to preserve the mind of peace and a life of non-violence.

The oracle deck has been written for this purpose: to connect to a heavenly source to give guidance in the practical application of the 'universal laws of attraction', which further explain the spiritual laws and wisdom to help advance mankind's evolution. Through education and imparting spiritual knowledge, this goal is possible to achieve!

The artist identifies herself closely with the spirit of nature and all other magical beings that exist in this fragile world. She sees herself as a messenger that represents Mother Nature. This role has a purpose to support, promote and teach environmental awareness. Her path is dedicated in helping the Deva kingdom from being further destroyed. This magical world could become lost forever, if mankind continues to abuse the environment. Within nature are natural medicines for healing, which further support the ecosystem of life.

CHAPTER TWO

INTRODUCING COLOUR MEDICINE FOR THE 21ST CENTURY

Ancient civilisations worshipped the sun as an energy source of light and colours that has healing powers for all of life.

The therapeutic use of colour and teachings can be recorded back to Egypt, Greece and Rome. A physician in the 11th century, a Persian called Avicenna, created a systemised approach to healing and medicine, in the tradition of Hippocrates. He wrote about colour as a symptom of disease and as a treatment.

The Egyptians that built the pyramids placed their healing chambers to the highest point to the heavens to access the universal energy of light rays for healing. The ancient civilisations were a highly advanced race that worked in the field of astrological sciences, quantum physics, universal laws, metaphysics, mathematics and sacred geometry. They also knew about earth sciences using crystals, gems and herbs for healing the body.

In the 18th century, scientists and philosophers were more concerned with the material world and focused more on medicine for physical ailments with advances in surgery and drugs, than dealing with the spiritual and mental wellbeing of mankind. Colour therapy re-emerged in the 19th century with the work of Edwin Babett, who focused on the principles of light and colour in 1878. Most of today's understanding of colour has its foundation in the work of Sir Isaac Newton.

PRINCIPLES OF LIGHT

Colour is a source of energy and is considered to be an aspect of 'light'. When light passes through a transparent prism, the light becomes refracted and reveals several bands of colour. Each band of colour vibrates towards a specific energy field. Bright colours tend to vibrate towards a higher frequency. These colours make us feel warm and happy. Colour is energy, which can uplift and heal the soul of the human spirit.

The refraction of colour rays

Colour can harmonise and balance our chi and thus improve our life and destiny. Chi is our essence and our psyche. Without chi, we are merely flesh and bones. Chi is the breath essential to maintain physical, environmental and emotional balance.

When colour is analysed in the field of science, these light rays can be incorporated to influence and change the body vibration within. These different waves of colour fields can help to rectify any imbalances, illness, disease and overloaded or blocked Chakras in the body. These colour rays may be invisible or visible to the human eye. These colour light rays can be applied to the body either physically or mentally through a visualisation technique and a form of meditation.

In this century, therapists are working closely with the healing powers of colour in psychological testing and physical diagnosis. The Lusher colour test was based on a theory that colour can stimulate the different parts of the nervous system which affects the metabolic rate and glandular segregations. The use of blue light has helped to treat neonatal jaundice and as a pain relief for cases of rheumatoid arthritis.

HEALING THROUGH COLOUR AND NATURE

The human body is alive with energy that flows in and through it. Chakras are channels through which the energy flows into our bodies. This chi energy is a universal life force that is found in all living and existing matter. Chakras means 'wheels of light' which are vortexes of subtle energy within the human body.

CHAKRA COLOUR CHART

8. The Angelic Realm (magenta)
7. Crown Chakra (violet)
6. Third Eye Chakra (indigo)
5. Throat Chakra (blue)
4. Heart Chakra (green)
3. Solar Plexus Chakra (yellow)
2. Naval Chakra (orange)
1. Base/Root Chakra (red)

A WAY OF BALANCE

Open and balanced Chakras help to maintain health, harmony and inner wellbeing. These energy centres feed and nourish physical organs with the energy they need in order to function properly. Every Chakra relates to a gland, which in turn feeds the specific organs of the body. These energy centres also connect to the emotions, mental and spiritual. Whenever these Chakras are stressed, blocked or overloaded, illness and dis-easement prevails.

ABOUT THE CHAKRAS

Each Chakra regulates the flow of hormonal activity in the glands which connect to the organs. If the flow of Chakra energy is stifled or slow, these vital organs suffer a depletion of energy thus becoming weak. Because our mind is also energy, our emotions and ideas can create stress in these Chakras. The Chakras are responsive to positive and negative thought patterns. If we are unhappy, worry too much or live in fear, doubt or confusion, then these Chakras become affected and may close entirely thus creating dis-easement. It is necessary to transform these damaging thought patterns to positive life affirmations to allow Chakras to flow freely with energy thus maintaining health and inner wellbeing!

By taking responsibility for our energy, we open doors to greater awareness, growth and development. Each Chakra resonates towards a specific vibration and a colour field.

COLOUR AND THE BODY

The human body and all living things have an 'aura'. This energy field extends outside of the being and radiates outward. The aura contains many different flows of colours depending on one's mood, emotions and personality of the soul. This living energy field tends to change depending on what a person is experiencing through life. If a person is angry, the aura will contain a lot of red. The colour red indicates frustration, pent up energy, passion, vitality and strong willpower. Other colours represent different interpretations, for example yellow is for joy, upliftment, wisdom and connects to the intellect of a person's mind.

The colour yellow is related to the sun; its energy makes us feel warm, happy and revitalising. By introducing the colour yellow to the body, one's chi can be improved, especially if someone is depressed or sad.

The body organs vibrate also to a specific energy field. These energy bands relate to a specific colour as illustrated in the diagram image on page 183. The body is a spiritual vessel and is made up of energy. The body contains seven energy Chakras which are called 'the wheels of life'. Each Chakra vibrates to a specific colour energy field. Located above the head exists the angelic realm which is the eighth energy vortex that connects to the Crown Chakra. This energy source contains the entire rainbow light. The dominant colour found here is magenta which relates to unconditional love.

CHAPTER THREE

THE SPIRITUAL PSYCHE OF COLOUR FOR MANKIND

Colour is a living energy and has a language of its own. Colour plays a vital role in our lives which can influence our mood, mental state and physical wellbeing. The food we choose to eat, the clothes we wear, the interior colour of our homes etc. can reveal many aspects about ourselves. Understanding the significance of colour can enhance our lives beyond recognition.

Colour is important for mankind's survival and for all other living species that are found on the earth. Without colour and light in this world, nothing would be able to survive! Colour is like 'fuel food' for the mind, body and soul. It is essential to work with all colours from the rainbow light to maintain good health, inner wellbeing and harmony.

Every colour is symbolic and represents a universal language which affects mankind physically, mentally and spiritually. The purpose of the Colour Medicine Oracle Card Deck is to understand the meaning of colour for the use of healing the Chakras that are found within the body of mankind. The interpretation for every colour and Chakra is listed as follows:

 **The colour red connects to the Base Chakra.**

The symbolic meaning of red: helps to ground oneself as it connects to the physical plane called earth. This Chakra identifies one's willpower, the physical side of life and the material plane. The colour red represents our life, blood circulation and passion.

The spiritual plane: deals with energy and strength. It helps to bring in regeneration and purification. Our willpower sits in the Base Chakra. This area is called the 'kundalini energy' which is like a serpent that remains dormant until it is required. Through the practice of meditation this kundalini energy can be aroused to rise from the Base Chakra to the Crown Chakra. Enlightenment and a level of spiritual awakening occurs when this has been achieved.

The mental meaning: the colour red deals with the material side of life and one's own power and authority. Sometimes a sacrifice is necessary for a change which can bring in stress and chaos at the same time.

The emotional meaning: red is a bright colour of the light spectrum which can represent heat, fire and energy. When we feel stuck or in a rut, red can be used for motivation to help direct the willpower for manifestation. Too much red may mean an overabundance in the material world. Red is symbolic for wanting order, structure and security in life.

The physical representation: the colour red is for blood and works with blood circulation, veins and stimulation for energy flow. If there is a depletion of iron in the blood, this can bring on exhaustion and fatigue. It can also influence blood pressure to become low. When feeling in a stressed state, blood pressure could become high and create hypertension. Red can represent fever symptoms with sweats, swelling and heat.

Red is important for sexuality and fertility. For women especially the menstrual cycle needs to be balanced, working with ovaries and for reproduction of birth.

Any lower back pain and trouble with the hips can be associated with the colour red.

 **The colour orange connects to the Navel Chakra.**

The symbolic meaning of orange: works with one's divine self, harmony, art and beauty. The monks of Buddha wear orange robes to represent divinity.

The spiritual plane: orange gives insight for a person looking for a purpose in life. They want to belong to something. This Chakra colour is the doorway of intuition, which is to trust one's feeling to help guide our life.

The mental meaning: orange represents wisdom and philosophy. It taps into the art of learning patience and perseverance in our life.

The emotional meaning: following a gut feeling for intuition, if a person has experienced some kind of shock or trauma in their life, this Chakra will be blocked, stressed and off-balance.

The physical representation: the Chakra connects to the lower bowel, spleen, gall bladder and kidneys.

 **The colour yellow connects to the Solar Plexus Chakra.**

The symbolic meaning of yellow: represents the sun, happiness and joy. In Chinese medicine this colour stands for the earth.

The spiritual plane: yellow represents seeking knowledge through study and the ability to learn which helps to stimulate the intellect and the mind of a person. This is the Chakra of our spiritual power connecting to the light.

The mental meaning: too many ideas can bring in confusion. Being unrealistic and unfocused can create disharmony. Too many ideas can lead to distraction, procrastination and anxiety. The mind needs to have order and balance. It is important to de-clutter the congestion of thoughts; by introducing meditation this can help to achieve clarity, focus and direction.

The emotional meaning: the ability to find inner joy, happiness and contentment in life. The opposite can relate to fear, negativity and a lack of trust. Yellow connects to nervousness, cowardice and self-worth issues. Having low self-esteem, no confidence or to doubt oneself could correlate with depression. Yellow can bring in optimism and positivity to uplift the mind.

The physical associations: works with the Solar Plexus Chakra. Organs in this region are the stomach, digestive tract and the liver. The nerves, nervous system and the skin are also related to these areas of the body.

The colour green connects to the Heart Chakra.

The symbolic meaning of green: is for peace, healing and love. The colour associations with green in other areas include: a new direction in life, money, growth, creativity, freedom, harmony, nature and the Deva kingdom.

The spiritual meaning: green is for healing, finding one's own truth and compassion. Follow your passion from your heart for creativity and the love of nature!

The mental meaning: to analyse with logic and to be practical when making decisions. Sometimes we have to learn to compromise and to become flexible in life. To give and to share certainly helps to benefit the community.

The emotional meaning: to honour, to love and to be open-minded. By being kind and generous to others is good karma! Diplomacy and freedom of speech is essential for self-respect. If discontented in the heart, this can mean envy, jealousy, hatred and bitterness.

The physical associations: the heart, lungs and the thymus gland.

 **The colour turquoise is a 'new age colour' that connects to the Heart and Throat Chakra.**

The symbolic meaning of turquoise: connects to the 'Age of Aquarius', when Atlantis, an underwater city, was built. This advanced ancient civilisation worked with crystals, light, wisdom and ocean law. The colour turquoise is linked to the sea, the dolphins and the creative arts.

The spiritual meaning: an advanced civilisation that came from space and time working with the universal law.

The emotional meaning: listening to the heart to find the truth and the ability to trust intuition. To be optimistic, a counsellor with sympathy and empathy. The area of creative media communication and teaching.

The physical associations: the heart, throat, lungs, thymus gland, upper neck, bronchitis and asthma.

 **The colour blue connects to the Throat Chakra.**

The symbolic meaning of blue: is to bring heaven down to earth for peaceful communication.

The spiritual plane: blue represents psychic protection which connects to Archangel Michael. Blue is the colour of divine light, offering support and assistance when required.

The mental meaning: represents leadership, diplomacy, authority and the ability to trust intuition for higher guidance.

The emotional meaning: to feel secure, being at peace with oneself, tranquility and relaxation.

The physical associations: open communication for the Throat Chakra, the thyroid glands, the immune system to fight against infections, and controls metabolic rate which helps to maintain weight balance.

 **The colour indigo blue connects to the Third Eye Chakra.**

The symbolic meaning of indigo blue: is the ability to see into the unknown which is called clairvoyance; the 'All-Seeing Eye' which penetrates into the truth of the matter. A Mystic with psychic abilities. Working with one's visions and ideas, indigo blue represents the moon, the consciousness and the supernatural.

The spiritual plane: the gods of Egypt are associated with indigo blue, bringing forth wisdom and knowledge.

The emotional and mental meaning: to feel at one with all that is. To be alone, wanting space for peace and for rejuvenation. This colour can relate to issues with a dominant father figure. Feeling the blues and mood swings which can lead to depression.

The physical associations: connects to the pineal gland, eyes, ears and forehead. Tension headaches and eye problems.

 **The colour violet connects to the Crown Chakra.**

The symbolic meaning of violet: is about transmutation, transformation, spirituality and healing. The Crown Chakra works closely with the angelic realm. The violet flame represents Saint Germaine. To serve and to heal is a noble service working with the divine world of light from heaven and bringing it down to the earth plane for healing.

The mental meaning: the need to be careful of stress. Violet is excellent for meditation and relaxation. This colour vibration helps to open up the Crown Chakra for higher guidance and trusting psychic impressions.

The emotional meaning: too much worry and anxiety. Difficulty with living in the now, worries about finance and the material side of life.

Feeling at a loss, suffering in silence, abandonment, alone, grieving and isolation.

The physical associations: the Crown Chakra is above the third eye, the temple, the brain and the top part of the head.

 The colour magenta connects to the eighth energy vortex which sits outside the body above the head called the 'Angelic Realm'.

The symbolic meaning of magenta: represents compassion, empathy and unconditional love.

The spiritual plane: at any time ask the angels of the light for support, guidance and healing energy. The Chinese goddess of compassion is known as 'Kuan Yin'. She represents a female deity who is similar to the Buddhist's philosophy of being caring and seeking no harm onto another. Magenta helps to open and activate the heart centre to receive love. This colour deals with feminine intuitive energy.

The physical associations: the hormonal system and the reproductive organs magenta helps to transform negative energy for love is pure, innocent and has a holy divinity that is given freely by the source.

This angelic colour represents unconditional love for self and for others. It can be used to help to nurture oneself for healing within. Also helps to balance the feminine side of ourselves which is 'Yin' in energy. Connects to all health carers to give support, a caring attitude and to respect oneself.

CHAPTER FOUR

CREATING THE COLOUR GEOMETRY CHAKRA MAPS

The Colour Medicine Oracle Cards contain eight geometry Chakra maps that have been created and channelled with the help of Tao through the artist.

The art of geometry connects to the universal laws of space and time. These are powerful healing rays of lines that help to centre the Chakra for healing, to re-energise, for balance, harmony and to re-align the meridian lines that are found within the body of mankind. Geometry works with quantum physics, mathematics and metaphysics.

The star systems found within the universe connect to a grid-like energy net that interlock to create balance and harmony. This is a gravitational pulling system that works on distance, weight and volume.

These geometry Chakra maps have been designed to infiltrate every Chakra with a flow of colour vibration that acts accordingly to the healing level of receiving an attunement. Every colour ray has a unique light vibration according to its level of brightness, intensity and darkness. The brighter the colour, the higher in chi energy flow. Darker colours have a lower vibration, being slower in speed and have a low sound ratio.

Every card connects to a field of light energy which we absorb through the eyes to bring in balance, healing and harmony for the body. Every Chakra in the body is distinct from each other. Every energy centre has a specific vibration and a colour flow. Linked to each Chakra is a sound, emotion and a symbolic shape.

The Chakra maps created in the oracle card deck are used for healing, tapping into the higher consciousness for mankind. An explanation of the Chakra geometry symbols are listed as follows:

 **The first Chakra symbol which is called the Root Chakra or Base Chakra formulates a square symbol.**

The square is symbolic of the earth. It gives stability, security and practicality. The four lines can be drawn to create a cross which taps into the four elements of fire, wind, air and water. The cube is about being solidified. The four represents the makeup of mankind being spiritual, physical, mental and emotional. The square symbol is the foundation for one's courage, willpower, flight or fight to survive, and helps to activate direction and to work through challenges in the material world.

The musical note sound connecting to the Base Chakra is Do.

 **The second Chakra which is the Navel Chakra is represented by a triangle, which is the symbol of fire.**

The three lines represent trinity, which is the spiritual identity of the Father, the Son and the Holy Spirit. Also the Father, Mother and God; Father, Mother and Child; Spirit, Soul and the Mind; and Super consciousness, Subconsciousness and Consciousness. It also represents the pyramid of eternal life which points to the upper heavens and stars that are found within the universe.

The musical note for this Chakra is Re.

 **The third Chakra which is the Solar Plexus Chakra is represented by a circle, which is the symbol of eternity and immortality of the soul.**

The circle that is the sun that gives us life, strength, support and warmth. It is a powerful symbol for protection. All planets in the universe are round. The Divine Source, God energy and the haloes of the saints and angels have the figure of the circle above their head. The circle is the universe – all in one.

The musical note for this Chakra is Mi.

 **The fourth Chakra which is the Heart Chakra is represented by the symbol of the heart.**

The symbol of the heart relates to truth, honesty and communication. The elemental energy is air. This Chakra is about unconditional love, peace and tranquility. Love is the purest energy in the universe, and it helps to transform negative energy. The heart is the centre of our being for self-respect, integrity and diplomacy. This is the seat of one's power. Remember that to be vulnerable is actually a sign of strength not a weakness. Listen to the heart for guidance and empowerment.

The musical note for this Chakra is Fa.

 **The fifth Chakra is called the Throat Chakra and is represented by the symbol of a triangle pointing downward to the heart and on top is a cone.**

The symbol reflects a multifaceted diamond that has been cut many times. We have the ability to communicate on all different levels of creative expression, feelings, visions, thoughts and ideas. This is the bridge to work from the heart and the mind as one. It is important to be honest and truthful in dealing with others. We have to voice our opinion to utilise wisdom, tact and diplomacy. To offer peace and messages from heaven we utilise the throat Chakra. The cone reflects the light and purity of one's expression and the intent of every spoken word.

The musical note for this Chakra is So.

 **The sixth Chakra is called the Third Eye which is represented by the symbol of two pointed triangles; one is a reversed mirror image of the above triangle pointing downward.**

This symbol relates to the universal laws of 'as above so below'. It relates to truth and wisdom. The world of spirit sits above and the material world is below. The image looks like a spear and is known as a 'God head'. In the middle of the circle sits a triangle with another small circle which represents the 'All-Seeing Eye'. Every being has a sixth sense and a level of intuition. This is a centre of trusting what we see and feel in life. It helps to connect to one's ideas and vision to manifest into the material plane.

The musical note for this Chakra is La.

The seventh Chakra, called the Crown Chakra, is represented by a circle with an eight pointed star.

The circle opens up to the cosmos for higher guidance and for protection. The star reaches out to all corners of the universe. We are all living in one source which also deeply reflects one's own spirituality in life. If we activate this centre it will help for healing, bringing in beauty, opening up to the divine and connecting to the realm of spirit. This Chakra is the psychic doorway of receiving impressions, divine intervention and future predictions.

The musical note for this Chakra is Ti.

The eighth Chakra which sits outside the body above the head is called the angelic realm.

The symbol for the heavens is represented by the Star of David. This powerful symbol represents light, eternity, protection, divinity, peace and power. It connects to our highest self which relates to the truth of the image that we see within ourselves. The upper triangle world is spirit and below the lower triangle is the material world. The two come together to create balance, harmony and universal consciousness; the seed of light connecting to space and time. It is also known as 'the wishing star'; when activated it can bring in prosperity, happiness and joy. The rainbow rays of colours in the symbol bring in balance, healing energy, upliftment harmony and peace of mind.

The musical note for this highest energy centre resonates to the universal stars of light consciousness, which are all notes in one!

Red Chakra Banner by Sylvia Meissner designed by Art House Reproductions. >

CHAPTER FIVE

COLOUR REPRESENTATION OF EVERY CHAKRA

Colour representation for the Chakras which connect to the glands and organs that are found within the body.

Base Chakra: Red in colour.
Meaning: Sexuality and willpower.
Chakra location: At the base of the spine, front and back.

Function of the glands: These are the reproductive glands. They are the primary sex organs that are found within female and male bodies. The testes in the male contain the production of reproductive cells called spermatozoa and a hormone called androgen. The male produces testosterone which affects hair growth, enlargement of the larynx, deep voice, development of other glands, the prostrate and seminal vessels.

In a female the hormone is called oestrogen. In the female the primary organs of production are the ovaries. Oestrogen helps to regulate cyclic changes in the uterus, including the protection and nourishment of a developing embryo.

Physical organs: The sexual organs, the rectum, blood circulation, leg veins, lower colon, bladder, hips, legs and feet.

Navel Chakra: Orange in colour.
Meaning: Divine creativity and emotional feeling.
Chakra location: In the pelvis region just below the navel area.

Function of the glands: These are the adrenal cortex glands. This pair of glands sits just above the kidneys. They help to regulate the body's metabolism, electrolytes for sodium, potassium and water balance. The glands supply sex hormones which are secreted by the gonads. The adrenals prepare the body for flight or fight. The adrenalin becomes affected by fear, anger or stress. It helps to get the body activated for any activity. Usually heart attack victims need a shot of adrenalin to restore normal breathing which becomes effective immediately. These glands also support muscle tone, including the peristaltic action in the intestine. Also adrenalin is beneficial for asthmatic conditions.

Physical organs: The bowel area, intestines, the kidneys, the spleen and the reproductive organs.

Solar Plexus Chakra: Yellow in colour.
Meaning: Spiritual power and self-worth.
Chakra location: In the middle of the stomach area, just below the sternum.

Function of the glands: This is the pancreas. The pancreas is attached to the duodenum and produces both external and internal secretions. The external secretion, called the pancreatic juice, contains alkalising bicarbonate and digestive enzymes. The internal secretions are hormones called insulin and glycogen. These two secretions help to regulate carbohydrate metabolism, including the use of glucose by tissue cells as well as the formation and conversion of glycogen into glucose for the liver.

Physical organs: The stomach, digestive tract, liver, gall bladder, nervous system, the skin and the small intestines.

Heart Chakra: Green in colour.
Meaning: Unconditional love and truth.
Chakra location: In the middle of the chest area of the lungs near the heart.

Function of the glands: This is the thymus gland. This gland is a lymphatic organ which is located in front and above the heart. This organ helps to manufacture antibodies and controls the body's immune system during childhood years.

Physical organs: The heart muscle and lungs.

Throat Chakra: Blue in colour.
Meaning: Communication and peace.
Chakra location: In the centre of the neck near the windpipe.

Function of the glands: This is the thyroid gland. This gland helps to regulate basal metabolism, which is the speed at which our body burns and uses cells. It is important for one's growth, development of teeth, enhances muscle tone, aids in mental development and helps to promote the functional activity of the gonads and the adrenal glands. Mostly all of iodine is found in this gland, which affects weight loss, nervousness, rapid heartbeat, weight problems and dryness in the skin. The thyroid gland also secretes the growth hormone called thyroxin.

Physical organs: The structure of the neck, outside and inside, the vocal cords, mouth, teeth, jaw and tongue.

Third Eye Chakra: Indigo blue in colour.
Meaning: Intuition and third vision sight.
Chakra location: On the forehead, in the centre above the two eyebrows.

Function of the glands: This is the pituitary gland. This gland is the size of a pea and is attached to the hypothalamus, which is located at the base of the brain. It is a master gland of the endocrine system; it manufactures hormones for all other glands that are found within the body. These hormones control skeletal growth, secretion of milk by the mammary glands, maturation of the reproductive cells, growth and development of the gonads, activity of the thyroid, blood pressure and pancreas function. The pituitary gland regulates all growth for the body.

Physical organs: The eyes, skull, sense organs, brain and the nervous system.

Crown Chakra: Violet in colour.
Meaning: Spiritual awareness and the psychic gateway.
Chakra location: The crown of the head.

Function of the glands: These are the pineal glands. These organs are found within the brain, and secrete melatonin, the hormone that regulates sleep patterns, into the blood stream.

Physical organs: The brain, nerve centre for pain, nerves and the spinal cord.

Angelic Realm: Magenta in colour.
Meaning: Unconditional love and protection.
Energy centre location: Sits just above the head outside the body.

Physical senses: Connects to one's highest self and for divine guidance supported by the angelic realm.

This divine source of energy can be used for healing and to connect with the source of universal unconditional love. This is the pathway of service and helping others, a form of sacrifice and asking for protection with the support of Archangel Michael and Saint Germaine.

Saint Germaine abstract by Sylvia Meissner

ABUNDANCE

CARD MEANING: *To be fulfilled of a desire or an achievement that will require great riches of the world.*

The word 'abundance' can mean plentiful supply. Every person has a different viewpoint about abundance that meets their own desire. It does not have to be associated with money or material goods; for example a fisherman may want an abundant supply of fish to feed his family and to support the local community.

We all have the power to manifest what we want in our lives, as long as it is practical. Through the use of prayer and meditation, one can seek the spiritual pathway to manifest abundance for one's life. The rule to attract abundance is to resonate with the desire – you have to feel it – and visualise the outcome; however, be positive and have fun in the process. Remove any negative thinking or doubt. Be open, believe in it and allow your heart to be free from any limitations. Feel worthy of receiving, think of prosperity and have good ambitions in mind that can help the community. We must learn

< *Universal Cosmic Light Dream*

to share this abundance with others; as the saying goes, 'a good deed done deserves another'.

AFFIRMATION: 'I accept and honour my true worth. I am ready to receive abundance in every way!'

MEDITATION: Visualise the main colour red, followed by other colours of orange, violet and magenta for this task to activate high energy to bring in motivation. Direct the willpower from the Base Chakra to the upper realms of spirit. Open the Crown Chakra, which is the doorway to the angelic realm. Connect with your vision, ideas and inspiration to guide your way. Bring that desire and intent to the Earth plane. Work with it to manifest abundance into your life.

MAIN CHAKRA HEALING COLOUR:
Red.

ACCEPTANCE

CARD MEANING: *The action of consenting to receive or undertake something offered.*

The universal law that extends to every living being on the Earth is to work through any challenges or obstacles as life lessons for learning that can assist one's soul for spiritual growth.

The web of life presents itself from the past and into the present to balance karmic debt from our own individual actions. It is important to forgive ourselves and to bless those that have sought us harm, pain or hurt in any way in order to create a new path of life that resonates with a higher level of 'Divine Love' for positive attraction.

One should always be careful with the power of thought. If we practice an attitude of being more mindful with compassion, empathy and wisdom, it will allow us to become free from the law of karma. Our role in fate has already been pre-ordained prior to the soul entry to the Earth plane.

We cannot alter the path of destiny, as mankind is here to participate on this playground of the Earth as a school for our life lessons that connect to all things that are material, including living energies that can offer us a level of heightened perception and many other worlds for self discovery.

Life can always be challenging along the way; perhaps you may leave a job because of an illness, or the company makes you redundant which is out of your control? In searching for a job, you may feel disadvantaged because of your mature age? You decide to start up your own business which turns out to be the best course of action! You may find that you become accepted into a new group, winning a prize or signing a document for an inheritance? It is important to accept unconditional love for oneself, inside and out, with self respect to help find a loving relationship or supportive friendships. If a health issue cannot be altered or healed, then we have to accept the limitations and try to be positive and happy within ourselves to get the most out of life! If we hold onto negative thought patterns, the process for healing will take longer and can create more stress, depression and feeling sad for oneself.

For further reading in this area please read: 'You Can Heal Your Life' by Louise L. Hay.

AFFIRMATION: 'I feel worthy and at peace to take up a position of acceptance of who I am.'

MEDITATION: Close your eyes and visualise the bright little stars in the universal night sky. Accept that you are also one of these dazzling shining lights, as we are all connected to the source. Work with trust and have more faith within the spiritual law of order. Just be who you are and flow in the cosmic web of magical dreams to find yourself! Visualise your spirit floating in the beautiful Aurora Borealis of healing colours from the Divine that will lift your soul for serenity and for bliss!

MAIN CHAKRA HEALING COLOURS:
Yellow, green, blue and indigo blue.

ACTION

CARD MEANING: *When we want something, we need to act upon it!*

If you are thinking about what you really want, then we have to meet it half way. If we just wait, become lazy, or are simply not motivated, then the situation or issue will not fully come to the fore. If we are worrying too much, this can create more stress – so it is always best to act upon it. You may have a goal to achieve, need to finish a project, want a new job, start a course, want a commitment, need to lose weight, give up an addiction, visit the dentist etc. To initiate a direction, we need some form of positive output from your entire being.

It is no use relying on others to do it for you; as the saying goes, 'you are your own master to create your own reality in life!' If you are feeling worthless or powerless, then take a course in an activity that focuses on empowerment, strength, courage and belief! You can really do it, have more faith in yourself and try to do your best. If you have this attitude you are more than halfway there to gain with what you want. The time has come for you to take action! No matter what happens you will feel great once you action it! You have taken a brave step forward and this will give you more confidence. So be proud and take one step at a time.

Time does get away and before you know it, it could be too late! So don't hang back or get distracted – go for it!

AFFIRMATION: 'I direct my willpower to attain the best possible result!'

MEDITATION: If you feel a bit sluggish or tired, the best way to re-energise your whole being is to visualise the colour red. You may find a piece of clothing with this colour that you could wear on the day. The Base Chakra Geometry chart can also be used for visualisation as this will help to direct your willpower to create a shift (see page 39). If you feel stuck or in a rut, get moving with the colour red!

MAIN CHAKRA HEALING COLOUR:
Red.

ANGELIC GUIDANCE GEOMETRY MAP

CARD MEANING: *We live in a world filled with love and light.*

Every soul has a guardian angel that looks after us at all times. When we need help, call upon them to assist us in working for our highest good. We have to ask for their assistance, however; this will not be freely given unless destiny has allowed it to occur. The law of spirit cannot intervene with karma. Every soul on the Earth plane must work through their own challenges, issues and lessons for the purpose of soul growth.

Angels can give us support, unconditional love, healing energy, courage and protection. When an angel is around us, we can feel a tingling sensation, as well as a beautiful, warm and loving energy. We can connect to this powerful energy of love and compassion to transform any negative or heavy energy.

Fill your Heart Chakra with unconditional love and send it out to those in need. Learn to meditate and to still the mind to gain access to the higher world of spirit. Become aware of your dreams as your angel may be trying to communicate a message to you through them.

Look for a sign – it could be a white feather, a lucky coin or anything that represents a good omen.

We are never alone in this world. Loved ones, family members that are deceased, friends and even pets can become guardians and protectors in our lives.

AFFIRMATION: 'I call upon the angels of the light for love, support, courage, protection and for divine guidance. Amen.'

MEDITATION: The art image has a pentagram in the circle; an ancient and magical symbol for protection and wisdom and is shaped as a five-pointed star. It has a supernatural power that connects with the universal light, the Holy Spirit and a divine God force. This wishing star can be activated to bring joy, prosperity and happiness. The rainbow light expresses balance, peace and harmony. It is helpful with any kind of illness or dis-easement that is found within the body that requires attention for healing.

Visualise a 'rainbow light' coming through the Crown Chakra and see it moving down to the Base Chakra. If this is difficult to visualise, absorb the light through the eyes by focusing on the art image. You can also sit in natural sunlight for at least fifteen minutes and ask for this beautifully coloured light to filter through your entire inner being.

MAIN CHAKRA HEALING COLOURS:
All the rainbow colours.

BALANCE

CARD MEANING: *The symbol of the oracle card represents yin and yang energy.*

These two opposing energies meet at a point of balance. The laws of the universe decree, 'as above (the heavens) so below (the earth)'.

Heaven and earth are interconnected as one. Mankind is a 'light being' derived from the source of the cosmos. We were born on earth to learn about balance for the environment and to share with all living species.

We should only take what is necessary for survival and replace or replenish what has been taken away. We have to give respect towards this planetary eco-awareness that explores the universal law of 'balance within life and nature'. Mankind must take responsibility for the welfare of our precious planet. The evolutionary path for mankind is dependent upon living in a healthy and a sustainable environment.

On a daily basis, balance in life is necessary; all work and no play can create a feeling of being off balance. Working long hours can create exhaustion, no energy, stress, tiredness, depression and other illness related health issues. Take some time out for leisure activities, eat a variety of balanced, nutritious meals, drink plenty of fresh water and get some fresh air and exercise.

AFFIRMATION: 'My life is in the flow and I am in the centre of the universe to maintain equilibrium and balance for every day.'

MEDITATION: Visualise the 'yin and yang' art work image through meditation for balance. The colours of light blue and indigo blue will help to open and balance the third eye and the Throat Chakra. The third eye centre explores vision, ideas, stimulates clairvoyance, psychic awareness and often leadership abilities. The Throat Chakra delivers verbal expression and communication from beyond.

Another simple exercise to achieve balance is to visualise the white light from the universe and bring it through the Crown Chakra then to the Base Chakra. Sit in this zone for ten minutes; this will help to open, re-energise, heal and keep every centre in balance. When these energy vortexes are in alignment, the maintenance of good health and inner wellbeing can be achieved along the way.

MAIN CHAKRA HEALING COLOURS:
All the rainbow colours.

BASE CHAKRA GEOMETRY MAP

CARD MEANING: *The Chakra centre that connects to our willpower, strength and courage, as well as the structure and order in our lives.*

This Chakra is powerful as it symbolises what we can manifest from our true desires to the outer world.

The Base Chakra is red in colour and is associated with our sexuality, passion and vitality. We need to have this Chakra open and flowing in order to help direct one's own goals in life. This can include any other achievements or activities that you would like to do your best in.

Within the Base Chakra is the 'kundalini fire', which is our life force energy. Whenever we feel the need to take action, for example in fight or flight which is our survival instinct, this Chakra gets fired up. Stored here is a serpent-like energy that springs into action when required. If this Chakra is blocked, overloaded or stressed, it can make us feel sluggish, tired or we feel a lack of motivation in our daily life.

When we suppress anger, frustration, hatred or hold onto fear, this Chakra becomes affected. To help heal this centre, seek counselling and visualise the colour red in meditation.

The Base Chakra is symbolic of the earth; it is the root star which helps to ground the individual in a practical way to help pursue any life goals.

AFFIRMATION: 'I follow my willpower and passion to create my true desires in life.'

MEDITATION: Visualise the Base Chakra Geometry Map in your mind to heal, harmonise and to activate this energy centre. The Geometry Map of the Base Chakra which is a square in a circle, connects with the elemental aspects that are found within us.

This energy taps into fire, earth, water and air. Like a compass in the centre of the square which represents a 'Symbolic Cross', these four aspects connect to our physical body, mind, spirit and soul – which we can now work with the outer material plane to help manifest our true inner desires.

MAIN CHAKRA HEALING COLOUR:
Red.

BELIEF

CARD MEANING: *Follow your instinct and trust in the process of divine guidance. The challenge is to believe in yourself and your skills, abilities and talents.*

Stay focused and committed towards your goals in life. Have the confidence and faith that things will turn out for the best. Negative thought patterns can get in the way of achieving something great!

Visualise a positive outcome, surrender and release your fears – let the universe guide you to your highest good. The laws of the universe, such as 'cause and effect' work with synchronicity. When the timing is right, everything will fall into place. Be patient during this waiting period and do not give up! Be strong and work through any challenges or obstacles that may unexpectedly come your way.

Remain open minded, stay optimistic and flexible – as a solution is always available through creative thinking.

AFFIRMATION: 'I work with the power of having the inner confidence, faith and trust to create wholeness in my life.'

MEDITATION: Visualise the Solar Plexus Geometry Map for inner power, self-worth, self-esteem, joy and acknowledgement of your talents.

MAIN CHAKRA HEALING COLOUR:
Yellow.

BLISS

CARD MEANING: *To be content; having peace inside and joy in your heart.*

Fill your inner being with happiness; spend some time with nature, go out and play! The flowers of the earth created from the divine have powerful healing energies to uplift the soul. Enjoy the sweet perfumes of beautiful aromas and rainbow colours from the angelic world that have been created for us to enjoy!

Bright colours help to stimulate, activate and to improve one's own chi energy. These vibrant colours help to bring in more energy for the body. We can feel re-energised, uplifted, relaxed and become more motivated.

If you are feeling tired, exhausted or unhappy – replenish your soul with a bright colour! Wear something colourful that will lift your spirit, or place some beautiful flowers in your home to feel inspired. Do things that you enjoy – try something creative to get your ideas going for inspiration.

Life is for enjoyment; take each day as it comes. Dance to the magic and the divine power of Mother Nature!

AFFIRMATION: 'My life is full of fun, laughter, bliss, happiness, love and joy! I feel the warmth inside my soul – like the radiant sun!'

MEDITATION: Visualise the colour yellow for joy, followed by other colours in the rainbow for balance and for inner wellbeing.

MAIN CHAKRA HEALING COLOUR:
Yellow.

BREAKTHROUGH

CARD MEANING: *A situation or an obstacle that has been left unresolved is about to be confronted and dealt with in a fair manner.*

The wheel of karma moves forward to release anything that has been stuck in the flow of life. Stay focused as a positive outcome is on its way. Get ready to reap the rewards of hard work and consistent effort. This is a well-deserved achievement, so celebrate the good news!

In life we have to face many different challenges that test one's own faith, skill and abilities. Every experience is a stepping stone for learning; there is no such thing as a mistake.

The journey through our life is to master certain lessons that we have consciously requested in the process of incarnation before entering the birth plane. Any obstacle becomes a test for every human being living on the earth. This planet is our Earth School of learning that provides valuable pathways for soul growth. It also serves as a way to work through any karmic debt that has been created from previous lifetime experiences.

During this holistic process, we get to gain a level of understanding and wisdom. This discovery of finding one's self contains a depth of richness for the soul where every individual will get to gain out of living life to the fullest potential.

We can share our own experiences to help others in need. When we begin to work with compassion, integrity for oneself, honesty and empathy, we can create a better world.

When we learn the art of mind concentration through meditation, we begin to trust the inner world of cosmic silence. This exercise helps to connect to one's own highest self for intuitive guidance. It is important to learn temperance and patience along the way, followed by tolerance for others – this is certainly a virtue to behold.

AFFIRMATION: 'Life is always about accepting a challenge! I am prepared to learn and to grow along the pathway of karmic lessons!'

MEDITATION: Visualise a seed and plant it in the ground. Now water it liberally with kind and loving thoughts. Nurture it as if it was one of your own beloved treasures. See it grow tall and strong, reaching towards the heavens!

MAIN CHAKRA HEALING COLOURS:
Red and green.

CELEBRATION

CARD MEANING: *Having fun whilst enjoying a special occasion.*

Celebrate the good news: this is a time of opportunity and luck! An unexpected event where someone 'out of the blue' could make you an offer that is too good to be true. Someone from your past that you have helped out before could return with a kind gesture. If you feel that you have some leprechaun luck, buy a lotto ticket – you could end up winning some money!

Whatever the special occasion is – an engagement, a birthday, a new home, business success, a birth of a child, overcoming an illness, a new job etc. – go out and celebrate the good news!

In life, we can experience many 'ups and downs' like a roller coaster. Nothing in life remains the same forever. This cycle of karmic reward brings in unusual events that offer good tidings and blessings – so be ready to accept them!

When we have accomplished a certain task, a difficult challenge or achieved a personal goal, we should celebrate this well-earned achievement!

It is important to recognise the effort, time and the energy spent on working towards our goals!

We should reward ourselves for the hard work that we have accomplished!

Share this special occasion for it can also help to inspire others with their own personal journey towards success and motivation. We need to work with focus in order to attain our goals.

AFFIRMATION: 'I am open to receive blessings that come my way – I am ready to celebrate the good news!'

MEDITATION: Visualise the Solar Plexus Geometry Map for joy, fun and spontaneity!

MAIN CHAKRA HEALING COLOURS:
All the rainbow colours.

CHAKRA HEALING

CARD MEANING: *When any of the Chakra energy centres in the body become stressed, blocked or overloaded, it is essential to re-balance these Chakras through a healing session. These energy vortices need to be open and free flowing to maintain good health and harmony for our wellbeing. We cannot see these subtle energy centres with the naked eye, however through a technique called 'Pendulum Dowsing' using a crystal, we are able to diagnose the energy flow of each specific Chakra that is found within the body.*

Every Chakra centre must flow clockwise in an open and circular motion above the body. The pendulum will demonstrate the flow; if the Chakra is stressed, the pendulum will move horizontally across the body or not move at all. This indicates a malfunction with the energy flow that is found within the energy centre. If the pendulum moves in a large circular motion above and over the Chakra, this indicates that the centre is overloaded, has too much energy and is being depleted out of the body.

If the pendulum moves all over the place in different directions, then this Chakra is unbalanced. If the pendulum moves in an anti-clockwise direction the flow of energy will have to be re-aligned. Seek advice with a spiritual healer who is able to balance these energy centres through a healing session.

These Chakras connect to our emotions and our mental, spiritual and physical wellbeing. If these Chakras are found to be out of balance usually some form of illness or a level of dis-easement can be found near the affected Chakra. Any negative thought patterns can also affect the flow of harmony. Every Chakra is connected to the various glands and organs that are found within the body.

This energy network that is found within the body is our vital life force. Every centre must be open and flowing to maintain balance and harmony for good health and inner wellbeing.

AFFIRMATION: 'My body is the temple for my soul; I must learn to nurture it and to take responsibility for my inner wellbeing.'

MEDITATION: Consult a professional spiritual healer to re-align and harmonise the Chakra centres that are found within the body. After the session, you can use the 'Rainbow Light' meditation technique listed on page 36 on a weekly basis to maintain the Chakra's balance and harmony.

MAIN CHAKRA HEALING COLOURS:
All the rainbow colours.

CLIMATE REVIEW

CARD MEANING: *The world is experiencing unusual weather patterns caused by global warming, which has been attributed to man-made causes.*

The Earth is a natural living energy system. When Mother Nature becomes abused or disrupted, we create an environment that becomes out of balance. All other living species on the earth will also become affected. Any temperature changes on a global scale will have a direct impact on the welfare of our precious planet.

Any environmental problems that have been caused by mankind must be closely scrutinised and a solution must be found to rectify the problem. A new vision to heal the planet must be taken into consideration as a priority in order for mankind and other species to continue living on the Earth. A management system has to be implemented on a global scale. All nations must work together to create a healthy ecosystem for our precious environment!

Mankind must learn to work in harmony with all other living inhabitants that are found on our Earth.

What ideas do you have to help to resolve the situation? The people of the world can become united to help our fragile environment called Mother Earth. Write to local governments and get a petition going! We need to share this message of environmental concern with the world!

AFFIRMATION: 'I seek no harm unto any other living species as I also learn to respect the environment; I will nurture and protect our precious planet called Mother Earth.'

MEDITATION: Connect with the Heart Geometry Map and the Angelic Realm Geometry Map. You can choose any one of these art images for meditation. Fill your entire being with these colours and send unconditional love and healing rays to Mother Earth.

MAIN CHAKRA HEALING COLOUR:
Magenta.

COMMITMENT

CARD MEANING: *To honour and to become more involved with something; an obligation that has a mutual understanding where it can help to benefit all parties involved.*

We may be in a long term relationship that needs some kind of direction for the future. It is time to go deep within your heart to find the answer. If you feel happy and content, then this is the right decision to make. Love will grow and deepen, as long as both parties are dedicated to making it work.

It may be a time for a business venture to commit to an agreement. If you feel that this is beneficial for your purpose, then step into it with courage, strength and belief.

You may decide to get a pet – this is a lifelong commitment that needs to be honoured and must be respected.

We must take care to look after our family, especially elderly people who need love, support and care for a healthy lifestyle. In regards to having children, we need to look after them with the same respect.

Sometimes to make a commitment can be very confronting, however this is always going to be a part of our journey in life. It is best to work through this challenge and to let go of any fear or doubts. Most things in life can be healed and important lessons are going to be learned along the way.

If you try to divert away from the situation, it may come up again somewhere else on your life path – until you get to understand that it can be of benefit, in whatever way that may be.

You may look at your health, and change to a dietary plan that will help you lose weight. Again this situation needs to be committed and acted upon with your own willpower to achieve the possible results for longevity, inner wellbeing and for happiness!

No matter where we direct our attentions in life, somewhere this obligation will always turn up on our own doorstep – so to speak.

AFFIRMATION: 'I make the right choices which are based upon the truth found in my heart; I am happy with this decision which I will honour in the best possible way.'

MEDITATION: Connect to the Heart Chakra Geometry Map on page 87 and the Solar Plexus Chakra Geometry Map on page 149. Visualise each of these one at a time and absorb the colours through your eyes. The colour yellow is for your self-respect, spiritual power, confidence and joy. The colour green is all about your truth, and the direction your heart wants to follow; relax and let it all unfold without controlling anything. You will find the answer which relates to the wisdom of your choice. If you are still unclear, go to the Confusion oracle card on page 57.

MAIN CHAKRA HEALING COLOURS:
Yellow and green.

COMPASSION

CARD MEANING: *The ability to listen and to connect with another without being judgemental.*

When we can relate to another human being with empathy and an understanding of how they feel, we begin to formulate a bridge of healing for the other. We can share our life experiences with others by being open and honest with communication. During any difficult times in our life, we don't have to do this on our own. Good friends have the role of offering selfless love and are willing to help in any way possible, which we should kindly accept.

Compassion is about unconditional love for all things and sentient beings. To become a Good Samaritan does take effort, kindness, tenderness, and spiritual awareness. All human beings on the earth have the right to live harmoniously with all others.

The time has come for mankind to shift his/her spiritual level of consciousness to the Heart and the Crown Chakra centres. Through these two higher spiritual energy zones, we can focus on embracing universal love, compassion, empathy, humility and to experience brotherly love for another.

We need to transform the world to bring in peace, harmony and to activate a life of non-violence whilst working with environmental awareness. In Eastern philosophy, the Chinese goddess of compassion and mercy is called Kuan Yin. Ask for Her help at any time to transform a situation that needs healing and forgiveness.

AFFIRMATION: 'My heart is open to receive universal love, comfort and peace. I share these blessings with the world!'

MEDITATION: Sit in a quiet place and visualise the cosmos filled with bright stars. Bring the rays of the light from these stars through the top of your head called the Crown Chakra, and then visualise the energy moving down into your heart. Connect to the laws of balance – 'as above, so below' – and with the figure eight as in the art image of Kuan Yin in infinity of light.

MAIN CHAKRA HEALING COLOURS:
Orange represents wisdom and divine creativity.
Violet for spirituality and psychic connection.
Red for grounding and energy.
Magenta for unconditional love from the angelic world.
Gold for protection which has been placed as yellow in the Chakra Bar Code on the oracle card.

CONFUSION

CARD MEANING: *When the mind is all over the place and has no peace or rest. Not being able to switch off when necessary or simply having too many ideas all at one time.*

The brain cannot function correctly if we find it too difficult to unwind or we become distracted from being involved in too many activities. If the brain is in constant overdrive with too much thinking, we can end up having a meltdown.

When the mind becomes cluttered with too many thoughts, it can make us feel bogged down. When we cannot see a direction or a way out, we need to bring in focus and clarity. A very good exercise to help the mind is to learn the art of meditation.

This is a mind exercise which helps to develop a level of concentration; thus from a state of chaos and feeling anxious we can find peace and inner tranquillity. Meditation is a therapeutic tool that is wonderful to use at any time that also helps to facilitate mental alertness and order for the mind. Regular meditation can become beneficial to retain good mental health and longevity for the body.

Too much stress and worry can create the opposite as a mental sickness for the mind, where it can create disruptive chemical balances in the brain. Let go of any negative thinking, remain optimistic and try to see the positive results in life. Get on top of it by finding the inner world of silence, which is a wonderful journey to embrace. It helps us for memory recall, dream analysis and psychic awareness.

Tapping into meditation can help to give us insight into the world of ideas by working with visionary concepts and inspiration to guide our life. Thoughts are like little energy balls that have been created by our mind – which we can use to manifest our desires to the outer material plane. All busy people would benefit from meditation as this will allow to bring to yourself a form of relaxation, energy and rejuvenation all at the same time.

When we feel confused, we need to break this repetitious cycle. It can make us feel trapped and hopeless. The mind needs to be focused and clear to direct our conscious thoughts toward what we want out of life. If the mind is scattered, it will be certainly difficult to achieve anything! The law of creation is simple; for example, when planting a seed into the ground it must grow out of the soil and reach up towards the light!

Our mind is a reflection of who we are; we all create our own reality!

Sometimes the mind can play monkey games with us. If we have fear, doubt or hold onto negative thinking, we tend to manifest a pattern of false illusion that comes with no holding power. We need to have a strong belief system, to be positive followed by joy in the process of working with our true intent. It is up to every individual to take control of their life destiny. What we make out of life stems from our own conscious thought patterns.

Mental depression can become a health problem when the mind is not in balance with our own emotions, feelings, soul truth, heart and spiritual self.

AFFIRMATION: 'I listen to the inner workings of universal consciousness to gain clarity, insight and to have peace of mind.'

MEDITATION: Visualise the colour violet to open the Crown Chakra which is the psychic gateway. Let go of any stress, fears and worries. Now move to the Solar Plexus Chakra (this is the stomach region) and visualise the colour yellow for joy. From there move to the Base Chakra and visualise the colour red. We are in the process of 'Rolfing' your energy network from your head down to your feet. This will help to bring in balance. Now walk along the earth with your bare feet for grounding. You should find yourself feeling heavy, balanced and centred.

MAIN CHAKRA HEALING COLOURS:
Red, yellow and violet.

CREATIVITY

CARD MEANING: *Open up to the world of imagination and inspiration.*

Work with ideas to create something: write, paint, draw, decorate, bake a cake etc. Do anything to get the right side of your brain to function! Take some time out to play and have fun. Do those things that give you joy, follow your passion – anyone can become creative.

Being in the flow of creativity gets us to solve problems, which make us feel good. When we feel relaxed, we enter into a zone of higher consciousness connecting to the spiritual world of enlightenment. When we learn to focus and concentrate within this creative process, the mind becomes inspired with lots of ideas. We have unlocked a new world to follow by controlling and blocking out chaos from our own mind to find contentment, bliss and peace within.

Work with your dream state and visions that connect to the third eye, to discover new ventures for creation. What you see around you on Earth is Mother Nature; a divine energy of beautiful creativity that has a purpose. The colour of the sky is blue, which represents heaven. The

< *Paradise Desert*

colour of the grass is green for rejuvenation and healing. Everything that you see has a symbolic identity, a message and a meaning.

Work with your gifts and talents, as we are also a source of divine inspiration.

AFFIRMATION: 'I am open to the source of divine creative flow by tapping into ideas and inspiration that will help my life in every way.'

MEDITATION: Find a quiet place close to nature, sit on the ground and open your mind to hear the surrounding environment. Get your sensory organs working to smell the air! Feel the light on your face, let go and explore the colours that you see in your third eye for healing. Listen to the song of nature and become one with the heartbeat of the earth.

MAIN CHAKRA HEALING COLOURS:
Orange, green and turquoise.

CROWN CHAKRA GEOMETRY MAP

CARD MEANING: *This chakra is the gateway for psychic awareness.*

When this centre is open, one can receive higher guidance from the angelic realm. We can connect to our spiritual teachers, ascended masters, guardians and higher beings of the light.

The Crown Chakra is violet in colour and is located on the top of the head. The purpose of this Chakra relates to spiritual unfoldment, which allows a connection to the God force. The Crown Chakra explores psychic ability and heightened perception. This energy centre also relates to the mind. When our daily lives become too fast-paced, if we tend to worry a lot or feel overworked and tired with no time out for relaxation, this centre can become blocked or stressed. The physical symptoms are headaches, anxiety, and tension in the neck and shoulders. Mankind is a spiritual being where balance concerning work and play is necessary to maintain good health. Through meditation, this Chakra can assist to calm the mind, relax the body, create peace, stillness within and rejuvenate the spirit with cosmic healing.

AFFIRMATION: 'The path of inner knowing helps to guide my way. I trust and listen to my intuition.'

MEDITATION: For universal healing visualise the Crown Chakra Geometry Map. Let the colours flow through your eyes for relaxation, rejuvenation and for peace of mind.

MAIN CHAKRA HEALING COLOURS:
Violet and magenta.

DISILLUSION

CARD MEANING: *Thought patterns of denial; convincing yourself that the outcome will come good when it will not happen that way, leading to speculation ruled by feelings of fear and insecurity.*

Get to the truth of the matter and find out about the real facts of any situation to prevent false hope, a loss, confusion or further misunderstandings. It is easy to talk ourselves into something when we want it so badly. Becoming complacent and lazy is an easy way out. Hoping that things could change for the better but living in another reality that does not connect with the truth of life. This can be a way to try to protect yourself from failure, a reality that's too hard to deal with or not wanting to confront a situation that has been around for a while. It is a feeling of fear that holds us back when we don't want to look at the situation as it really is. If you have been living your life this way in your head, it is time to change and take courage. These old patterns that you have certainly outgrown now need to be conquered!

Our mind is powerful and thoughts create our own reality. Negative thinking cannot be converted by wishing all things to come good or for the better. Now you need to transform these thought processes into clarity, meditate and let go of fear! Burn away this self-created mind rubbish, take control with positive action and believe in yourself!

AFFIRMATION: 'The time has come to find the truth in all things, I can see clearly the veil of illusion which now can be confronted with honesty and determination to find the right path of choice!'

MEDITATION: To gain clarity for the mind find a quiet place, then ask your angels to show you what is real and what is not. Visualise yourself in a glass dome that no one can penetrate. You are being protected from any negative influences from the outer environment. Allow your mind to de-clutter and visualise a clock with its hands moving around at a slow pace.

This distraction will help you to clear your mind and to bring order with your thoughts. Release any negative thinking and transform this energy with a positive affirmation. Most important is to forgive yourself, let go of the past and move forward with a fresh outlook in life!

MAIN CHAKRA HEALING COLOURS:
Red for willpower, yellow to release fear and to bring in confidence and indigo blue for heightened awareness through the Third Eye Chakra.

EXPLORATION

CARD MEANING: *Expand the mind to discover new worlds and other possible realities!*

If you want to find a deeper meaning about life, take some time to research into the mysteries of the unknown.

Ancient knowledge has many hidden secret pathways to find, to learn and to help discover more about oneself. A spiritual seeker will want to understand the universal laws to get more out of life. There are many other spiritual topics that can be researched into the area of esoteric sciences.

These subject matters include metaphysics, quantum physics, philosophy, philanthropy, mysticism, Buddhism, Tao, Zen, theosophy, vibrational medicine, crystal healing and the list goes on …

Mankind is here for learning; it is best not to become ignorant otherwise we will miss out on the richness of what life has to offer in return. Any of these topics will help to give us more of an understanding about the human race, our evolution, the plight of nature and the world we live in.

Once a seeker finds the path of 'enfoldment' this journey will never end. We will continue to learn and grow. The Creator has given us a chance to explore these hidden paths to find ourselves, which has a purpose for spiritual advancement, soul growth and enlightenment. We are all children of the light but some of us have lost our way. Become open and flexible with your mind, as a new adventure awaits you.

AFFIRMATION: 'My spirit soars to new heights of finding my true path; I am willing to become a seeker of exploration!'

MEDITATION: A creative visualisation technique for 'Exploration' is to find a quiet place under the night sky. Get into a meditation state whilst sitting and begin to visualise the universe. Connect to the rays of light from the sun, the stars and other galaxies. Now bring this energy light source down through your Crown Chakra and then down to your feet. Enter into the zone of universal silence; this is a high rejuvenation exercise. This form of meditation can help to activate mental alertness. You should feel charged up instantly!

MAIN CHAKRA HEALING COLOUR:
Indigo blue.

FERTILITY

CARD MEANING: *When the female body is ready to conceive, the sperm from the male and the ovum from the woman ignite to become a baby.*

The process of cell division takes place over the next few weeks to create a tiny figure that looks like the beginning of a young born. A soul will be re-born into the earth plane, over and over again according to the karmic laws of previous incarnations.

The soul will choose its parents and origin of birth. A soul has to continue to work through karmic lessons for soul growth and for higher learning! The school of human life is interlinked with other souls due to karmic debt, obstacles to conquer, challenges and other issues that have to be resolved in the present life time. The soul follows a path of destiny, as it is already written in the chart of the stars which we call astrology of the heavens.

Fertility can also represent creative ideas or a new concept to work with. Allow new ideas to germinate and trust in the flow of receiving divine guidance! If you have been trying to conceive, good news is coming, as a child will be born in the present year!

The news of falling pregnant could be unexpected. Be cautious if not planning to have a child.

AFFIRMATION: 'My life is in the flow that helps to create inner harmony: I am at peace, filled with the joy that allows conception to take place.'

MEDITATION: For couples considering having children, visualise the yin (female) and the yang (male) energy coming together as one. Use relaxation techniques to reduce stress and worry, to help the process of conception. Balance and a healthy lifestyle is a priority for both parties involved.

MAIN CHAKRA HEALING COLOURS:
Red and magenta.

FLEXIBILITY

CARD MEANING: *To be impartially objective and open minded for any constructive decisions about a situation that may require adjustments or amendments to achieve the best possible result for all concerned.*

Learn to listen closely to another person's point of view before making any judgements or criticism, as this will honour a mutual respect for each other. By being unbiased from the start with an open mind, we can learn to filter all the information and facts before offering an opinion or giving any advice. Communicate your thoughts and ideas, as this solution will help to benefit all parties which are involved. Take your time to explain all the necessary facts to determine the best course of action. As the saying goes, 'two heads are better than one!' If a person becomes intolerant and overly too assertive, this type of behaviour can be observed as being brash and someone who is very set in their own way. If this person cannot be open or flexible, they could be abusing their own power for self-interest only to satisfy their own ego or acting without insincerity, which can further create a negative affect towards a situation. If you are in a relationship or living with others under the same roof, remember to be flexible with sharing any of the household chores and duties to maintain good manners, balance and harmony.

Could there be a new opportunity or a work project that offers more flexibility with work hours, shifts and including time off?

As humans living on the Earth, we must take care to nurture our precious planet before placing material profits ahead of destruction for the sake of greed, stupidity and mismanagement of land practices. We need to save our endangered species on the Earth, like the polar bears from mass extinction from global climatic change. As humans we have no right to dominate the planet, we must learn to co-habitat with all creatures great and small. We are all dependant on the Earth's resources for survival.

AFFIRMATION: 'There are no limitations, I am open and flexible to achieve the best possible outcome!'

MEDITATION: Visualise in your mind a beautiful forest filled with tall trees. Find a tree that you like and sit under its long branches that touch the sky. Place your feet firmly on the ground and with your back sit up against the trunk of the tree. Draw in the energy from the surrounding air, breathing in peace and universal love for your heart, mind and your soul. Connect to this inner world of silence to find serenity by connecting to Mother Nature. Soon a fairy from the tree will appear in front of your eyes to ask you to 'Bless our Mother Earth and to send healing loving thoughts to nurture our beautiful planet from further destruction!' The message is of hope and we would like to thank you for participating on this journey as a good will ambassador for our Planet Earth!

MAIN CHAKRA HEALING COLOURS:
Blue, indigo blue and violet.

FOCUS

CARD MEANING: *Part of the process to create success is to complete a task. During these stages, we have to make a consistent effort to achieve a desired result.*

The challenge is to persist, work quietly on your task and don't give up! When the mind is clear and focused, it is possible to manifest what we really want out of life, as long as it is practical.

Along the way we have to be determined by believing in our own talent, skills and abilities. Don't feel despondent if things get bogged down or become stagnant. Use visualisation to manifest the desired outcome. Have faith that it will happen. If we lack focus, it is difficult to bring about what we truly desire. Remember that thoughts are an energy source which resonate to the outer world that we live in. The law of attraction implies that one has to be positive to create success. We have to stay optimistic during the difficult cycles in our life as there is a saying, 'all things will soon pass.'

AFFIRMATION: 'My mind is clear with the ability to stay focused in order to achieve the best possible outcome!'

MEDITATION: The mind is a powerful instrument and we can learn to train it through meditation. Try to listen to the inner plane of silence, as this will help to activate a level of heightened mental alertness. When the mind becomes clear of clutter, we are able to bring in focus, clarity and ideas for direction. By using inspiration, this tool will help to guide our life in every way possible for harmony and peace.

Visualise the Third Eye Chakra Geometry Map for this mediation exercise.

MAIN CHAKRA HEALING COLOUR:
Indigo blue.

FORGIVENESS

CARD MEANING: *If anyone has sought you harm in any way, we must bless them with love and light! Connect to your angels and send out unconditional love from your heart centre.*

We need to forgive and to let go of the situation that took place, otherwise this negative energy binds us to that person. We have to move away from our past, whilst at the same time bringing in positive karma for the future!

If we hold onto anger, hatred or revenge, we end up hurting ourselves and also others. To be truly at peace, we have to reflect this same energy within. We have to learn to become a 'ninja turtle warrior'; the ability to control our own emotions from the action of others, whilst creating a shield of protection from harmful energy takes effort and practice.

To deal with anything that is confronting and uncomfortable makes us feel vulnerable and insecure. To combat this side of energy, we must learn the art of patience, diplomacy and tactful thinking.

To master this exercise, we have to learn tolerance for others. Sometimes we can be our own worst enemy; when we want something but it didn't happen we question things and why it seemed to go all wrong. Then we get disappointed and end up blaming ourselves. Maybe our expectations were too high or the goal became unrealistic? We like to condemn ourselves, a good example of self-sabotage!

Now is the time to rise above the problem, whatever it may have been. Face it with courage and strength. We have to deal with it, whether we like it or not!

Through gratitude and grace, we begin to transform the situation to find the right path of balance.

AFFIRMATION: 'I forgive myself and others who have sought harm in any way! I speak the truth followed by kindness and sincerity in my heart.'

MEDITATION: Visualise a pink coloured ray coming from the angelic realm into your Heart Chakra centre. Send out this beautiful energy to those that need healing in any way. Amen.

MAIN CHAKRA HEALING COLOURS:
Green and magenta.

FREEDOM

CARD MEANING: *To have no restrictions in your life, to feel uninhibited where any obligations, commitments or attachments have been removed from oneself.*

Sometimes we have these thoughts that go through our minds – how wonderful it would be to become 'detached'; to just let go and have less stress, and let any other unnecessary worries vanish into thin air!

To unravel any shackles that have kept us stuck or blocked from the past, now brings a welcomed sigh of relief – offering a new perspective and a sense of adventure! It is important to take some time out to get re-energised and to complete any unfinished tasks that have been placed on hold. We need to de-clutter our personal environment, so the new journey can begin! It will be necessary to take time for this process, so be patient and have faith that everything will fall into its own rightful place in creating order.

It is so easy to get caught up in a busy society where every day we tend to get immersed in other people's psychological conditions, their own emotional patterns of manipulation and demands that can drive us towards frustration!

If you have been feeling this way for a while, like 'the mouse on the wheel' not getting anywhere, then it is time to escape from this entrapment or habitual pattern. We need to analyse a way out to find a path of least resistance. Of course you have to be practical, as any ongoing commitments at present certainly need to be resolved without too much disruption or damage.

Find some support or help from another person, a friend, a family member or a group of like-minded people.

If you never seek to find or ask, you will never know.

If you have been so busy in your career and think that you may be reaching burn out or feeling depleted in energy, then you need to take a break from whatever it is that is causing the problem. Our moods can change with stress that can create sadness, having the moody blues or being quick tempered or angry – not a happy life!

No doubt our own immune system can become affected by our own emotional, mental and spiritual state, which places further strain on the body. Low levels of energy can result in dis-easement or not feeling balanced.

We need to honour our body temple, to nurture it and most importantly we have to respect ourselves.

It is ok to say 'no' without feeling guilty. The advice given here is to simply not to take it on. We need to place limits and boundaries on what we can handle. Open communication to explain these guidelines prevents us from any other misunderstandings.

Become free from these conditions as your own willpower and self-worth is being tested.

AFFIRMATION: 'No one has control or power over me; I am free to find my own true identity followed by the will of grace!'

MEDITATION: Visualise a beautiful rainbow water spring fountain. Now, stand in the middle of it and let the water droplets splash over your body like a shower to release any stress, worries and burdens away. Simply see them washing away … from your mind, your heart and your soul! If you like, you can use your own bathroom shower at home for this exercise. Water is powerful for cleansing and getting rid of any negativity.

MAIN CHAKRA HEALING COLOURS:
All the rainbow colours.

Sea Weedy Dragons

Weedy Seadragons are listed as 'endangered species' due to global climatic change. Rising sea temperatures are killing off the green grass beds and kelp which they feed on and use as their home for shelter. They are very fragile creatures and should not be handled at all as you may hurt or harm them. These days to see one is becoming rare, let's keep our oceans and waterways free from pollution!

FRIENDSHIP

CARD MEANING: *A close relationship or a special bond with another.*

This can also be with an animal, a group of people or even a child. These feelings are mutual and come with respect; we also feel comfortable to be in the same personal space with another. When we belong in a community group, we can all embrace working with friendship and helping each other. The saying goes, 'a good deed deserves another!' This merit on its own is worth the weight of gold! The world we live in is about sharing and giving. Friends are important; we can share the good times and lean on them in the difficult times. To maintain good mental health, we need to be amongst friends for support, laughter, communication and understanding.

If you feel that you are on your own, it is time to embrace a warm and loving friendship. Join a club to meet new people, accept social invitations, expand your network and embrace other activities. Surprise yourself and do it for fun!

AFFIRMATION: 'I am open to receive a loving and a supportive friendship; my inner soul reaches out to find what I truly need.'

MEDITATION: We are never alone in this world: we all have spirit helpers and guardians that are around us at all times. Loved ones that have passed over are also looking after us!

Find a quiet place to send out your loving thoughts and fill your heart with joy. Ask your angel to help you at any time. They can send healing energy for comfort and support.

MAIN CHAKRA HEALING COLOURS:
Green and blue.

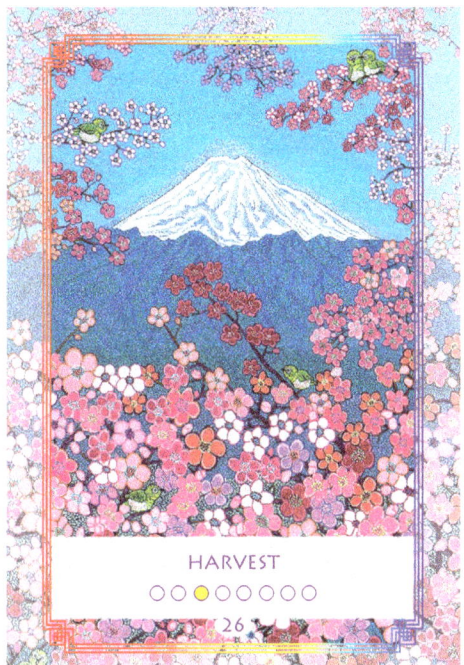

HARVEST

CARD MEANING: *If any of our efforts have been worthy, the law of cause and effect will be equal to the amount of energy expended.*

The time has come to reap the rewards from previous hard work! The road to success is always going to be a challenge. Celebrate the positive news and share this good fortune with others. Any project that has worthwhile ambitions will grow and expand. Any thoughts of negativity can create unfortunate loss and disgrace. If anyone has used an achievement for their own personal gain, for power or for greed, the karmic law will send back repercussions to the owner threefold. Be careful with your actions, sometimes they can speak louder than words! In life we all have to learn the art of giving and receiving.

The upper world of spirit, 'as above', and the lower material world, 'so below' which is the earth plane, has to be in harmony with each other. The human body is a spiritual vessel, wherein it is necessary to bring in balance from these two worlds that we all live in.

Through meditation we can link these two worlds together. We are moving into a higher plane of spiritual awareness and consciousness for mankind to relate and to understand. We all have the ability to manifest our desires, as long as it is practical and is for the highest good!

Reward yourself for the hard work done!

AFFIRMATION: 'I am ready to receive blessings; may good fortune be given, that I am able to share this opportunity also with others! Amen.'

MEDITATION: Visualise prosperity and send out positive and happy thoughts!

MAIN CHAKRA HEALING COLOUR:
Yellow.

HEALING

CARD MEANING: *As light beings, we are one with the universe! Open your mind to visualise the energy rays of healing given freely by the Cosmos.*

The rainbow colours of the light dance amongst the bright stars to give us joy and hope! Connect to these colours for healing; bring it through the top of your head and down to your feet! We are now activated to work on ourselves a form of self-help healing. You may receive one specific colour ray to work with for a particular Chakra that needs balancing for the body; go with the flow and trust in what you are shown. For example, the colour green is for the Heart Chakra, orange is for the Navel Chakra, etc. Every Chakra connects to the glands and the organs that are found within the body. A level of colour-healing can be implemented whilst working with our highest self and by working with this spiritual level of consciousness, we begin to become more in tune with the body. The mind, soul, physical being and spirit must be in harmony to maintain good health.

Seek a professional healer skilled with Reiki energy for any illness to bring balance to the body. Begin a class in healing, find a spiritual church; join a group of like-minded souls to begin a new journey!

AFFIRMATION: 'The universe is a divine source of healing energy for the mind, body and soul!'

MEDITATION: Visualise all the rainbow colours and bring them down through the Crown Chakra then down to your feet. Work with every specific colour that relates to every Chakra centre. After the session, ask for a colour that is relevant to your situation. You should receive a colour in your mind's third eye. Send this colour to the specific Chakra centre where it is required.

MAIN CHAKRA HEALING COLOURS:
All the rainbow colours.

HEART CHAKRA GEOMETRY MAP

CARD MEANING: *This is the heart centre of one's truth, desires, unconditional love, empathy and compassion.*

To attract love in our lives, we have to love ourselves first! This Chakra centre has to be open in order to receive love! Our heart contains inner wisdom that helps to guide us in our life. This is the seat of our inner power. Through courage, strength and self-respect, we learn to conquer most challenges along our soul journey.

The Heart Chakra connects to the angelic realm of unconditional love. This energy is pure, created from the divine to heal: to transform fear and negativity. Ask the angels for this beautiful energy for peace, contentment and to bring love into your own heart! Follow your heart to find direction. Most importantly be truthful upon speaking to others. Be gentle and kind to yourself. Tune into this heart centre to find a loving, giving and supportive relationship. We need more love in this world for harmony and peace. Spread the message of working with unconditional love for your community and amongst all nations of the world.

AFFIRMATION: 'My heart centre is open to receive love from the Divine!'

MEDITATION: Visualise the art image of the Heart Chakra Geometry Map. Connect with the colour of magenta for unconditional love and green for healing.

MAIN CHAKRA HEALING COLOURS:
Green and magenta.

INDEPENDENCE

CARD MEANING: *To be self-reliant, where we are not dependent upon another.*

To stand alone if necessary, having the strength and courage to believe in oneself! We all have the ability to control and master our destiny of choices. Follow your truth in your heart and take action! Get your willpower activated and fight for what you believe in! Act like a leader; approach the situation in a diplomatic manner, exploring all facts that are logical and practical. Work with your vision – guide others with this concept. Don't become too stressed if other people cannot understand the vision. The workings of the universe will help you to connect to the same soul consciousness's of people that will embrace and nurture with what you have to offer. Trust in this process and don't give up! Become humble along the way and others will assist you by showing friendship and respect. Every individual has come to this world for a purpose; to find and work with one's own inner talents and gifts. Be bold and independent, it's alright to be different!

AFFIRMATION: 'I have the ability to stand alone. I act like a peaceful warrior to create the goal that I desire!'

MEDITATION: Visualise the Solar Plexus Chakra Geometry Map for personal power, self-acknowledgement, to be positive and to find joy.

MAIN CHAKRA HEALING COLOUR:
Yellow.

INTEGRITY

CARD MEANING: *We have to respect ourselves and honour the truth of action in any given situation!*

The law of karma implies a responsibility of moral issues for mankind to understand and to obey.

We should never seek harm or hurt another, use any negative action, lie or seek ways of earning a living by dishonest methods. To steal, shoplift or any other kind of theft is already committing to a negative output in life, for example. The offender will have to deal with these serious karmic implications according to the time that will be given by the divine.

A bad deed done will gradually come back for the worse!

We must honour our true self-worth and treat others with the same respect. When facing any form of harm, injustice, intimidation or bullying, we need to be strong and stand up for our own rights. It is alright to be yourself and speak your truth. Honesty creates a path of balance and to happiness.

AFFIRMATION: 'The truth is in my heart – I respect and honour who I am!'

MEDITATION: Visualise the Heart Chakra Geometry Map for kindness, mercy and compassion. Allow your heart centre to find the truth for the right action!

MAIN CHAKRA HEALING COLOURS:
Green and magenta.

KARMA

CARD MEANING: *A universal principle created from the divine that explores a powerful energy exchange in the law of life with cause and effect.*

Every action of a soul transmits this energy to the outer world for it to return back to the sender. This karmic law of action and reaction must take place; no one can escape from this universal source. It is real: if one has committed a bad deed the energy of return will be threefold to the one that committed the offence. So become mindful of your thoughts, words and actions in this life!

From the moment a soul is born into this Earth-world, the journey continues to its departure of death to be returned back to the world of spirit and light. Every soul must be reborn to continue the path of karma, to settle any debts, to bring in peace and balance for unfoldment and enlightenment. A soul returns to the earth plane to continue the challenges and lessons for soul growth. The purpose for mankind is to work from a higher level of spiritual awareness that will help to advance mankind's evolution in life. Along this journey, the soul interacts with others also dealing with karmic ties from the past and also into the present life.

The process of illuminating karma can become a life-long journey. Finally when the soul has reached a higher plane of no return, it reunites with the divine power of One. This level of existence moves into the upper spheres of light and consciousness; a place of bliss, peace, eternal love and to no return!

The art of living with the law of attraction implies that whatever one puts out into this world, it will certainly be returned to its origin of source. To sow the right seed of action can create good karmic benefits. Blessings come for good deeds done! Be aware that negative thought patterns can create a level of dis-easement for the body. The mind, soul and spirit must be in balance to achieve good health and inner wellbeing. Positive thoughts help to extend towards longevity, peace and a happy life.

AFFIRMATION: 'I create good karma by being mindful of my actions!'

MEDITATION: Visualise 'The Karma Card' art image to focus your attention in the centre of the pink light radiating from the star. Go deep within this universal light of love to draw upon unconditional love and truth for your heart. It will set you free to work from a place of peace and honesty from your heart which creates positive karma in return.

MAIN CHAKRA HEALING COLOURS:
Orange, violet and magenta.

LIGHT CHILD

CARD MEANING: *The children that are being born in today's world have a mission to bring in love, healing, empathy and compassion for all living things.*

These are 'old souls' that have reincarnated from previous lifetimes to offer a pathway of spiritual service. They have a duty of sacrificial love to help advance mankind's spiritual evolution on earth. These 'light children' have come far away from other star galaxy systems which have connected to the pyramids of time. They will bring into this world new ways of teaching and learning. These subject matters will reflect the concerns in environmental science, quantum physics, metaphysical disciplines, theosophy, ancient teachings and practices, light technology for healing and creative engineering for the Aquarian age.

These 'light children' from the stars will be highly sensitive and imaginative. They will become creative inventive pioneers, gifted in the area of psychic work and will become powerful healers of our time. They will have a mission and a purpose for mankind living in the 21st century – to offer spiritual unfoldment and enlightenment.

These highly intuitive souls have another humanitarian task: to heal the world and end any conflict amongst nations, working with wisdom and diplomacy for peace.

AFFIRMATION: 'The path of enlightenment is to follow the light that is within my soul!'

MEDITATION: Read the Angelic Realm Geometry Map on page 35. Visualise this art image for wholeness, peace of mind and unconditional love for the world.

MAIN CHAKRA HEALING COLOURS:
All the rainbow colours.

LOSS

CARD MEANING: *Something has been taken away, misplaced or has become lost. We could end up losing a loved one, a person or a pet that was close to our heart, or an object has or may go missing.*

A loss is about to take place so watch your possessions, secure your home from theft, keep an eye on pickpockets that could steal your purse or wallet, stay updated on your bank accounts, park your car in a safe place etc. Be wary who is around you and what they want!

In business or any other venture – be careful, the warning signs have been evident for a while! Take heed of these messages to prevent a misfortune from occurring! We may feel scared, hurt, upset and sad. To accept any loss is going to be difficult, however life generally moves along in a way to replace what has been lost. It's important to grieve, talk it over with people that you know and care about. We need to openly talk about it; this is a positive way of dealing with the situation.

To incur any kind of a loss is unfortunate, however sometimes it can be for the better! When we get to a point of being overloaded by something, no matter what it is, something usually has to give! We can only try to understand and compensate for the divine law of action. With a new beginning, it gives us another opportunity to find a different way of thinking. The way it has been now offers a blessing in disguise. With nature there are many different seasons found within the year and we all have to adjust to the cycles of life.

AFFIRMATION: 'I view karmic principles as a natural process of life; I adjust to any given situation to rebuild a better future filled with love and joy! Amen.'

MEDITATION: Open the Heart Chakra to bring in unconditional love and peace. Visualise the colour green, with pink coming from the angelic realm. Work with the colour indigo blue for the Third Eye Chakra to stabilise the mind from depression. Now bring in the colour yellow for happiness and letting go of any sorrow!

MAIN CHAKRA HEALING COLOURS:
Yellow, green, indigo blue and magenta.

LUCK

CARD MEANING: *A windfall of something by fate and chance.*

You are about to receive a good omen from the heavens! A magical energy that brings fortunate tidings and blessings!

Luck comes to us freely; if any good deeds have been accomplished in the past and in the present, they will be returned to us. When we resonate with the feeling of abundance and joy in our heart, we can magically bring in our desires. The power of the mind has to be in a state of positive thinking! Our thoughts are like radio waves that send out messages to the outer world of matter. We have to believe to direct the willpower and visualise the subject to make things happen!

A new opportunity could present itself in an unexpected way. Luck is on your side, be humble and don't take the situation for granted! Be grateful for this God-given gift! Celebrate this joyous occasion!

If you want to create more luck in your life, find a horse shoe, an Egyptian scarab, a four leaf clover or get a citrine crystal and place it in your living environment!

AFFIRMATION: 'My inner world shines like a beacon of light. I am happy and grateful for any blessings that come my way!'

MEDITATION: Put your mind at peace and visualise happy thoughts! Let go of any worries, be positive and ask for blessings to come your way!

MAIN CHAKRA HEALING COLOURS:
Yellow and green.

MAGIC

CARD MEANING: *A supernatural energy which can be conjured up from the beyond!*

We live in a world filled with magic; everything you see in nature, the earth and the universe are all part of this beauty, filled with creativity and expression. In the earth are many different minerals that contain energy for healing! We are surrounded by these powerful elements of divine inspiration for important use. Sometimes mankind forgets their surroundings and takes these things for granted.

We see many miracles standing before us, like a beautiful rainbow, the sparkling stars in the night sky, a falling comet with its light trail, the colour of a flower, a singing bird, the colour aqua of the sea etc. are all here to observe and to see!

Become more aware about the precious environment that we all share and live in! Open your mind to the many possibilities of magic that exists around us every day. The hidden world of magic is there for everyone to see, by those who truly believe in it. We can manifest magic into our own lives by having positive thoughts, which can help to heal, uplift and bring joy!

We can ask for divine guidance to deliver some 'special magic' to help a situation for the highest good!

Send out a wish and it will be granted!

AFFIRMATION: 'I believe in 'magic' to make it happen!'

MEDITATION: Sit quietly somewhere in nature and visualise the fairies, elves and other magical creatures that exist in the Deva kingdom. Connect to this living world of magic!

MAIN CHAKRA HEALING COLOURS:
All the rainbow colours.

MANIFESTATION

CARD MEANING: *Believe in what you desire: in this process of visualisation send out positive thoughts. By using this simple technique of thinking, feeling and being one with the universe, the impossible can be made possible!*

The law of attraction is like a magnet that connects to one's own inner mind. The outer world of existence is the material plane, where we learn to play and to create what we want out of life. Go deep within your soul to find your true inner needs and desires. As we connect to this inner world, we now can manifest our wants to the outer plane of living consciousness.

Thoughts from the mind are powerful. We have to be careful with what we project to the outer world. In Buddhist philosophy it reminds us to become more mindful with our thoughts!

Negative thinking can create the same in return. For example, if we project some level of fear, insecurity, have self-worth issues, resonate with low self-esteem, or become nasty or mean, this energy will be returned to the sender. Something to seriously reconsider are our thought patterns. Any form of negativity can bring in misfortune, loss, struggles, obstacles, disbelief, ill health, bad luck, or even create accidents!

If you want to change your life for the better, we have to let go of fear and negative thinking! Work through positive affirmations to help heal and transform any situation that serves no more purpose for your life! We as human beings have come into this earth world to create our own reality!

The art of manifestation is a universal law to master. It is best to have a good intention that will also help to benefit others. This of course will become an added bonus!

AFFIRMATION: 'I have the ability to manifest my desire at any time; I have the power to change things for the better!'

MEDITATION: Visualise the colours of red, yellow and violet. Red is for the Base Chakra for willpower. Yellow is for the Solar Plexus Chakra for inner authority, joy and belief in oneself. Violet is for the Crown Chakra known as the psychic gateway that helps to transmit our thoughts to the outer material plane of consciousness.

MAIN CHAKRA HEALING COLOURS:
Red, yellow and violet.

MEDITATION

CARD MEANING: *A form of mind exercise to bring in tranquillity, a state of peace, ascending to a higher plane of consciousness, to re-energise and to relax the body.*

Meditation helps on all levels for the soul, mind and the physical being that we have come into this world of light. Good health is attributed to the body when all of these areas are in harmony and are balanced.

By introducing meditation into our lives, this enables us to achieve a level of self-help healing for any type of ailment. Attend a meditation class to learn the basic techniques and then you can practice in your own spare time. Working with meditation allows us to open up to the higher spiritual realms for universal energy healing. The universe is made up of 'chi energy' which is abundant; we can connect to this powerful source at any time.

Other aspects for using meditation is to help to bring in clarity, focus and for direction. When we tap into this universal energy source, we can also draw upon ideas and inspiration that helps to guide our lives. The mind does have to learn to de-stress, so the body can learn to unwind to feel re-energised. Thinking constantly can lead to stress, anxiety and other mind-related health problems, such as depression. Work with meditation to connect with the oneness of the universe, a flow of unconditional love and light energy for healing and for upliftment. When participating in any form of spiritual practice, it is important to work with a level of psychic protection. This simple technique is explained on page 199.

AFFIRMATION: 'I am one with the universe, love and light flows through my inner being for peace, healing and harmony!'

MEDITATION: At the beginning of this exercise, activate the psychic protection energy field.

The lotus flower is the symbol for meditation, relating to enlightenment and unfoldment towards a spiritual pathway. Visualise a place of peace – you can use the art image of the water lilies – become still and aware of your every breath. Breathe in love and breathe out any negative emotion that you would like to transform in your life.

Continue this exercise for fifteen minutes.

MAIN CHAKRA HEALING COLOUR:
Violet.

MOVEMENT

CARD MEANING: *A new journey is about to begin in your life. It is time to travel, embark on a trip into the country side, a change of residence or a move to a new location!*

This is an exciting moment in your life to accept adaptability, to change and to bring in adventure!

When we have outgrown a situation, the challenge is to find a new path. At this point in your life, if you feel things have come to a standstill or fallen into a boring routine – we need to have the courage to look for new horizons! Trust and work with this energy of transformation, letting go of old habits and rigid thought patterns.

Have the strength, fortitude and faith to leap into the unknown. Plan that holiday; pack your bags and go! Don't hold back, divine timing is on your side to connect to your path of destiny.

If you have been waiting for a reply, a form of communication or news is on its way! The outcome will be positive and enterprising! If you are feeling sluggish or tired, go outside to exercise the body! Any kind of movement is good for the physical being to maintain health, harmony and cardiovascular fitness!

AFFIRMATION: 'The time has come for a change with new surroundings: I am ready for adventure!'

MEDITATION: Visualise the colour red for willpower, strength and courage. Now work with the colour yellow for confidence and letting go of fear. The last colour to visualise is green to find a new direction that is guided by your truth in your heart!

MAIN CHAKRA HEALING COLOURS:
Red, yellow and green.

NATURE

CARD MEANING: *We have been blessed by the divine to live and to interact with this Garden of Eden that has been blessed on this sacred earth! Everything around us on this beautiful planet has a form, structure, colour and a purpose!*

We need nature for survival; it is our central pillar that gives us support, sustenance, medicine, oxygen, food, water, shelter, protection and clothing!

Nature is part of the ecosystem, which is fragile. Mother Nature plays a vital role towards the planet's harmony, constitution and balance.

When mankind creates any harm, disturbs, abuses, destroys or pollutes the environment, the ecosystem of life can become impacted in a negative way. It could take years or decades for the environment to heal. If the damage has been severe the environment may become unrepairable, even left barren, where no life can continue to survive!

Mankind must learn to replenish what has been taken out of the earth and implement balance towards their own needs. Nature, which is a part of Mother Earth, is warning mankind through global climatic change that the planet is out of balance. We need to resolve these environmental issues and problems that are occurring in today's world to have a clean and healthy, sustainable living space for now and into the future. Mankind must take responsibility for these living conditions, for the future survival of our own race and also for other living inhabitants that dwell on the earth.

Nature is a supernatural power, it cannot be controlled. The earth will find its own way to restore the balance and harmony for all creatures that are great and small.

AFFIRMATION: 'I respect nature and work with the divine law of order to bring in balance and harmony for Mother Earth!'

MEDITATION: Spend some time with nature for relaxation, rejuvenation, peace and tranquillity. Allow nature to touch every cell within your being! Connect to this magical source for healing, upliftment and joy. The earth, nature and the universe are all connected as one.

MAIN CHAKRA HEALING COLOUR:
Green.

NAVEL CHAKRA GEOMETRY MAP

CARD MEANING: *The Chakra centre for one's own emotions, feelings and intuition.*

This energy centre is orange in colour which represents our divine self and creativity. These aspects explore the expression of art, spiritual knowledge, philosophy and meditation. The Chakra centre is situated in the navel region of the body. The organs associated with this centre are the bowels and the kidneys.

When we don't express our feelings easily, or hold back and suppress our emotions, this Chakra centre can become blocked, stressed or overloaded. The colour orange is symbolic for shock and trauma. In life when we have experienced something dramatic like an illness, an accident, a separation, a loss etc. this Chakra can become affected. It can make us feel off balance, anxious and not feel like we're grounded.

A healing session with a professional spiritual healer for a 'chakra re-alignment' will help to bring in balance and harmony for the body. The navel Chakra connects to the adrenal glands which are our secondary source to supply energy for the body. If this energy centre becomes depleted or stressed, we may feel tired, drained and exhausted. It can also create a lower response in the immune system that helps to combat most symptoms of illness found within the body. Take some time out to bring in relaxation and work with the meditation exercise for the Navel Chakra centre.

AFFIRMATION: 'I allow myself to trust my feelings by finding the inner world of silence. I am open to the divine law of creativity and I am free to express who I am!'

MEDITATION: Visualise the Navel Chakra Geometry Map.

MAIN CHAKRA HEALING COLOUR:
Orange.

NEGATIVITY

CARD MEANING: *When our belief system becomes fear based, we can fall into a trap of becoming narrow minded. Living with doubt, feeling discontent with oneself or feeling unworthy can further contribute to loss and failure.*

Holding onto negative thought patterns within one's own mind can create disharmony, chaos, anxiety, anger, frustration, sadness and even depression. To hold onto anything that is not for our highest good can become destructive for one's own psyche and inner wellbeing.

The opposite of negativity is positivity. The law of manifestation works when one feels worthy about receiving, having confidence in oneself, being truthful and having peace inside; these feelings can create success! Send out happy and positive thoughts to manifest abundance for one's own life!

If your path is faced with negative challenges where you feel that you have no control and things are about to fall apart, this is the universe saying 'time to move on!' There is no turning back; follow this natural course of action. Feeling disappointed with a sense of loss is something to accept for now.

All events are pre-ordained; a new journey is about to begin, so let go of the old! Face this challenge with determination, courage and strength! Conquer your fears, move forward into your life having faith and trust to rebuild a better future that is going to be fulfilled with harmony and joy!

AFFIRMATION: 'I no longer hold onto any fears or negative thought patterns! I am in the flow of life, where happiness and positive thinking supports my desires!'

MEDITATION: Visualise the Solar Plexus Chakra Geometry Map to bring in upliftment, positivity and happiness for the soul.

MAIN CHAKRA HEALING COLOURS:
Red and yellow.

NEW BEGINNINGS

CARD MEANING: *A new journey is about to commence, leaving behind old habits and patterns!*

The time has come to move forward in life. Face this challenge gracefully – everything is going to be alright! If you are thinking about changing your job or want adventure in your life, now is the time to do it! Extend yourself because fate, luck and destiny are on your side! Don't get caught up in a boring or a mundane life; living in a rut for material means can only deflate the soul, it can make us feel empty which further adds to misery.

Break out of this repetitive cycle and try something new! Spread your wings, have faith and trust in the new life that awaits you! We can help to flow with this energy by clearing out any clutter in the home or office to make room for something new. In business be inventive, try some new ideas and explore other unknown ideas that can lead to expansion. Find a creative hobby or another interest to meet new people. If you are unhappy about your appearance, try a makeover or a new hairstyle. Revitalise a long-term relationship with a nice surprise, book a romantic dinner for two, organise a picnic or anything to have fun and romance to rekindle the love that has always been there!

AFFIRMATION: 'I have the power to create changes in my life, to revitalise my soul and inner being!'

MEDITATION: Visualise the colour red for willpower, strength and courage. By working with the Base Chakra Geometry Map on page 39, this will help to activate motivation. The moment of truth now awaits your actions to manifest change that is going to be inspirational and soul rewarding! Be at peace with colour of green that is connected to the heart chakra for rejuvenation and new beginnings!

MAIN CHAKRA HEALING COLOURS:
Red and green.

OBSESSION

CARD MEANING: *A desire, a habit or an addiction that has become out of control.*

This is when something of need that we desire all the time has become a focal point in one's own life. If this becomes detrimental to our own health and inner wellbeing, it is time to stop to review the situation and to find balance for a solution.

We need to rectify the issue, to bring a way of change for the better so that this habitual pattern can be confronted and properly managed. Too much emphasis in one area can create disharmony. All work and no play can create discontentment. Working long hours and not taking enough time out for oneself can bring in health problems. When the body becomes exhausted and tired, it can make us feel irritable, angry and depressed.

Sometimes we can be obsessed about something that benefits a healthy lifestyle, like exercise. Just don't go overboard – everything in moderation is the key to a happy and a rewarding life. Too much of one thing can suppress the inner chi energy which is found within our spiritual physical being. Taking things to the extreme level can become dangerous.

If we become obsessed about trying to force a desire to make it happen, this will not work! The law of attraction has to be in the flow; take a step back and visualise the outcome – it's like watching a movie from a distance! If we try to control a situation it will be as the saying goes, 'what persists actually will resist!'

AFFIRMATION: 'I seek the way of harmony to achieve the best possible result!'

MEDITATION: Open up to the doorways of heaven and ask for whatever needs to be changed, as this will be activated to find the path of balance and fulfilment in every way!

Visualise the Angelic Guidance Geometry Map for this connection and support on page 35.

MAIN CHAKRA HEALING COLOUR:
Green.

OBSTACLE

CARD MEANING: *When something becomes a hindrance or an impediment that creates a blockage on the path of free flow.*

This energy can become very frustrating! Life has many tests and challenges that have to be worked through patiently and diplomatically. It's no use throwing up your hands and deciding to walk away from it; that is all too easy. Don't give up, as it is now the time to resolve the issue! Get your mind to think outside the box; do some quiet meditation to reflect on the situation. Overcoming any obstacle on one's own journey in life is going to be rewarding! It will challenge your intuition, belief in oneself, courage and endurance to pass this test.

Any obstacle that has been presented to you is an opportunity for soul growth. Stay motivated as a solution to this problem will soon be overcome. Victory is at hand to the person that holds with wisdom, strength and trust. The outcome is positive which could bring in a new direction or other opportunities that we could not see before. A blessing comes in by surprise!

Life does not have to be a struggle. Send out positive thoughts and let go of fear. The higher powers of the universe can assist to create the flow of balance into your life again! Rise above the problem and work with this magical energy of 'divine timing', which relates to the laws of cause and effect.

AFFIRMATION: 'I embrace new beginnings to enter into my life – any challenges I encounter are for my higher learning and for soul growth!'

MEDITATION: Visualise the obstacle and transform it into your desire – see it vanish and dissolve! Ask for divine guidance – believe in the power of the mind!

MAIN CHAKRA HEALING COLOURS:
Red and blue.

PARTNERSHIP

CARD MEANING: *A union with another that formulates a close association.*

Such a relationship can connect to any area of one's life, whether it is a person that you love, a joint venture or working with another that can complement the business in any way. Accepting new concepts and ideas to harness the same vision can be a positive step for future growth.

The unity of two people, a group or organisation calls upon a collective level of consciousness to achieve a goal. Exploring new avenues for expansion will help as long as all parties involved are honest with each other, are flexible, have good communication and work equally with a mutual respect for each other.

A supportive bond can only strengthen to bring in success with whatever goal or desire that has to be achieved. The reason for coming together has a purpose. The challenge is to work in harmony; to synchronise in order to create something great! Along the way, we need to be patient and diplomatic. Express any thoughts, concerns or any other issues within this partnership! Be yourself; be open and free to do so!

AFFIRMATION: 'My vision connects to the right people to achieve the goals and dreams that I truly desire!'

MEDITATION: Visualise the artwork image 'Infinity of Light' which represents the universal law of 'as above – so below' on page 37. The colours found within the artwork of indigo blue, blue and white will help to open the higher spiritual Chakra centres that are located in the body.

The Throat Chakra is for creativity and open communication.

The Third Eye Chakra is for vision and ideas.

The white stars in the painting are for inspiration and divine guidance.

MAIN CHAKRA HEALING COLOURS:
Blue and Indigo blue.

PATIENCE

CARD MEANING: *Allow things to work through in their own time, to go with the flow without pushing or trying to achieve quick results.*

Sometimes in life we need to tolerate a delay. If we become impatient, we can end up making matters worse for ourselves and in turn can create unnecessary stress for others! Reassurance and focus is important to keep things moving on track. All projects will need to be evaluated and carefully prepared before making any final commitments. Take one step at a time to fine tune all the details to overcome making any errors or mistakes.

If you have not been very well, you will need time out to relax, to rest the body for healing and most importantly to pace yourself without getting angry or upset. Patience will be on your side as an alliance, if you rush this process it may take a longer time to heal and will take more effort for a full recovery! If starting a new business, take progressive steps for growth and expansion. This will need patience and future planning. If you have to study for exams, plan well in advance to achieve the best results. Start a few weeks prior to read over the information, as this will help to retain memory storage and to create more confidence. This will allow you to become more positive to manage also any fears or anxiety. Explore the tools of meditation as this is a mind exercise to help to bring in clarity, focus motivation and great for concentration skills. If you want to lose weight for health reasons, consider a long term plan rather than a short term fix. It is better for the body to make adjustments over a time period than losing weight fast. It will take strong willpower and discipline to accomplish a healthy weight goal. If you leave things to the last minute, rushing in a frenzy can create accidents, loss of balance and feeling clumsy. They say that 'patience is a virtue' which has to be learned and mastered.

AFFIRMATION: 'Time is on my side, I go with the flow to manage all of my needs.'

MEDITATION: Please work with the art work titled 'Golden Peridot Stargate II' for this exercise. Visualise yourself in the centre of the healing mandala of the Stargate. With your mind, concentrate on sending positive thoughts that are for your highest good to the universe. Stay focused and relaxed by connecting to the source. Give yourself a moment to feel the vibration of divine unconditional love for activating the Heart Chakra. Visualise your intent or a goal to manifest that will also help to benefit the community, healing the planet for peace and harmony, a clean environment and for mankind to show respect for all creatures great and small. Pray for divine blessings to come your way to fill your soul with great riches and accomplishments for success!

MAIN CHAKRA HEALING COLOURS:
Green, indigo blue and violet.

PERSISTENCE

CARD MEANING: *If we really want to achieve something, we have to put effort and time into it to make it happen!*

The challenge is to work through any obstacles, to remain focused and don't give up! Generally speaking in the flow of life, some situations can become difficult and trying. We have to remain positive, staying focused with our true intent to manifest what we want.

That can be easily achieved; follow the motto 'strive to succeed'! Release any fears or doubt and continue to be enthusiastic and optimistic! We have to believe in ourselves to create success! When any kind of obstacle is placed on one's path, this will test our faith, endurance and courage. By being persistent and standing up for our own beliefs, this will help to achieve our desire!

Expect some good news to come your way!

To create success, we need to have discipline, determination, followed by persistence.

At most times we have to use discretion, kindness, sincerity, honesty and diplomacy with others. To be focused and clear with intent can help to bring in positive results.

For example, to lose some weight, get healthy and fit takes time and discipline. Any form of study to advance your career or to give up a bad habit or addiction etc. needs persistence. This all takes effort, so stay focused and don't give up too easily.

AFFIRMATION: 'I will try to do my best to achieve any goals – followed by determination and focus.'

MEDITATION: Visualise the Solar Plexus Chakra Geometry Map for self-worth, confidence, inner authority, personal power, respect, letting go of any fears, doubt, and anxiety, and to bring in joy!

MAIN CHAKRA HEALING COLOUR:
Yellow.

PHILOSOPHY

CARD MEANING: *The study and theory of wisdom; an ancient knowledge that has a past history and a present system for social and individual behaviour.*

Allow your mind to become open and flexible to understand the learnings and the teachings of other civilisations. Every country explores a way of living, depending on its history, culture, religious rites and beliefs. To study theosophy helps to discover, to analyse and to review all religions of the world.

The art of living is to achieve harmony, happiness, peace, love and compassion. Eastern philosophies such as Buddhism, Tao and Zen explain the laws of nature and the universe that harness balance, good health and longevity in life. Take some time to explore the art of meditation to help to still the mind and become centred, allowing oneself to receive energy from the cosmos.

To learn about philosophy helps every individual to understand about the karmic principles of universal law. By working with wisdom, this will help to guide your life in a powerful way! Follow the light of intellectual perception; a spiritual journey to achieve a level of heightened awareness to bring in compassion and empathy for our daily ritual.

AFFIRMATION: 'Wisdom lights up the way in finding the truth about life!'

MEDITATION: Sit and become still, rest and relax. Connect with the universe and see yourself amongst the stars of the light. You may hear some humming noise that represent sounds and light waves of cosmic energy. Listen with your inner ear and dance with your soul to this harmonic magic!

MAIN CHAKRA HEALING COLOURS:
Orange and yellow.

PLAY

CARD MEANING: *Find the inner child within, be spontaneous and have some fun!*

Participate in a sport that you enjoy, attend a theatre play, sing a song, dance or do anything that gives you happiness and joy!

Take a stroll in the park with your beloved pet; animals also need to play and have exercise! This will help you to keep fit whilst at the same time will help to reduce any stress in your own life, so get some fresh air and sunshine to re-energise your whole being! It's wonderful to be surrounded by Mother Nature; we live in a world of beauty that sustains and nourishes our spirit and soul!

All work and no play can leave us feeling tired, moody, empty and drained. When the body becomes low in energy, any illness can attack the immune system. It will take a lot longer to recover so rest up and eat good food.

We need to work on balance for our own lives; that includes time for rest, pleasure and leisure. Do something creative; draw, paint, read, dance etc., anything that is fun and makes us feel inspired! We have to learn to enjoy life, so make time for fun and play! It doesn't matter what age you are and don't worry what other people will think! You are never too old to have fun, so find the sun in your heart and sing!

AFFIRMATION: 'I take time out for play, to have fun and to enjoy every moment!'

MEDITATION: Find a beautiful place in nature, sit and become still. Think of happy thoughts and release your worries over to the angels! All is well.

MAIN CHAKRA HEALING COLOURS:
Yellow, green and blue.

POWER

CARD MEANING: *To believe in yourself, to have courage and inner strength to combat any challenge!*

We must have respect for ourselves and have the ability to act with inner authority, followed by integrity. When we have to confront a situation, we need to speak our truth, to be firm and diplomatic. If we allow other people to treat us badly, we may be projecting to the outer world what we seem to be carrying within ourselves, which we can relate to having self-worth issues and low self-esteem.

Raise the standards that you would like to have for yourself; we shouldn't have to put up with it! This is a time of transformation to step into our own seat of power. Any person that portrays bad manners, it is best not to deal with them.

Someone could be abusing their own power by using the position of authority with deception, dishonesty and for their own personal gain. Being ruled by ego and driven by power or money can become harmful, if used for only selfish motives. This is someone who is abusing their own power! If you are dealing with a bully or a tyrant, be calm and communicate your truth. Your heart centre expresses honesty and unconditional love; we can use this healing energy for the highest good, this does have the power to transform any form of negativity! Feeling good about oneself is healthy and positive. We attract the same energy into our lives for wholeness, happiness and prosperity.

Don't be afraid of using your own power which can help other people in a constructive way. Treat them with respect and you will achieve more out of life!

AFFIRMATION: 'My inner power is my strength. I have the confidence and belief in myself to conquer any fears to move ahead in life!'

MEDITATION: Visualise the Solar Plexus Geometry Map for inner power, self-worth and for confidence. Let go of any fears!

MAIN CHAKRA HEALING COLOUR:
Yellow.

PRAYER

CARD MEANING: *The divine is a universal source of spiritual power to assist us in every way!*

By sending out a prayer to the Almighty, we are connecting to all that is. A request can be made to give us strength, hope, healing energy and for faith. Ask and it will be given! A prayer has to be made from your heart. Ask your angel anytime to assist you for your highest good to work through any kind of challenge.

A prayer has to be delivered with an honest intent. In times of hardship, feeling unhappy, in grief, not feeling well, unloved, alone, depressed etc., ask for upliftment to heal the soul! We have to extend ourselves to heaven followed by belief in order to receive a small miracle or some form of help. We also have angels on the earth that have a human form that are here to help us.

We are never alone in this world; we have loved ones in spirit, guides and angels that work beside us. They can give us unconditional love, comfort, strength and healing rays of light. No prayer will be left unanswered, so open up to this spiritual doorway of receiving, for support and guidance in every way!

AFFIRMATION: 'I send out prayers to ask for assistance in times of need. I thank thee for listening to my thoughts. Amen.'

MEDITATION: Whatever is happening in your life, find a quiet place for rest and solitude. Send out your thoughts with whatever you need, connect to the divine source; this is available for everyone, it doesn't matter what religion you have faith in.

MAIN CHAKRA HEALING COLOURS:
All the rainbow colours.

PROTECTION

CARD MEANING: *You are in a safe place where no one can seek to cause you harm!*

Every soul has a guardian angel that can offer comfort, peace, love and protection. The laws of spirit govern the angelic realm and who can assist a person in genuine need. Angels are not allowed to interfere in a person's life for karmic reasons. Only under special circumstances can they help, which is that they must be given permission and a blessing from the divine!

The angel for courage, strength and protection is called Archangel Michael. He is a powerful guardian who can transform any negative situation or harmful energy to conquer fear. His beautiful radiant energy rays represent an indigo blue light.

Visualise this colour all around your body to create an energy shield to reflect any dark, negative, heavy or low astral energy away from your being. By applying this simple visualisation exercise, it will help to keep your own energy field within a balanced level and prevent it from being depleted or drained. You can activate this 'protective shield' before leaving your home or at any other time.

The world is becoming a stressful place, and we have to deal with all forms of energy every day. People living in the busy world of today tend to carry a lot of distressing energy that comes with anxieties, mood swings, work and financial pressures etc. All of these annoying energies can affect our own aura fields. If you are working in a public place where you have to deal with people all the time, try to use this form of protection and see for yourself how well it actually works. It will make a big difference to use in your own life. You may not feel that tired when it comes to the end of the day!

AFFIRMATION: 'I call upon Archangel Michael to ask for protection, courage and for strength! Thank you for your support. Amen.'

MEDITATION: Another way of activating a powerful energy shield around your body is to visualise a white candle flame. Sit in this radiant magical energy of light, make a prayer and ask for protection from the angelic realm.

MAIN CHAKRA HEALING COLOURS:
Indigo blue.

PSYCHIC GROWTH

CARD MEANING: *A spiritual shift of energy that occurs within the body Chakras to connect to a higher source of light vibration.*

When these Chakras are open, we can receive a higher level of vibrational light energy for healing supplied by the universal source. The purpose for these centres is to become more attuned, thus helping to expand one's own level of sensitivity and to bring in further a level of heightened perception. Working from this higher plane helps to increase one's own psychic ability. The Third Eye Chakra which is called 'the all-knowing and seeing eye' further moves into the area of clairvoyance. During this transformative process, the Crown Chakra also begins to re-align with one's highest self to receive divine inspiration and guidance. This is the psychic doorway to receive messages from beyond the light veil.

During this cycle of growth, take time out to rest and keep up regular meditation. Go with the flow; this psychic shift is natural which will soon pass. The purpose for mankind's evolution in this world is for spiritual growth! By embracing a higher divine realm of consciousness, we can assist to work with peace, brotherly love, compassion, empathy, wisdom and mercy to make this world a better place to live in! As humans coming into this Earth world, we are also represented as 'light beings'. We are a spiritual vessel that represents a physical body that has a mind and a soul. Our purpose is to find the truth and the meaning for our life existence.

AFFIRMATION: 'I reach out to seek enlightenment; my soul continues this spiritual journey to find fulfilment!'

MEDITATION: Use the psychic protection and grounding technique explained on page 200.

Visualise the light rays from the sun – bring the light down through your Crown Chakra to the Base Chakra. The white light from the sun contains all the colours that comprise the rainbow light for balance and for inner wellbeing.

Relax and sit in this warm healing energy for about fifteen minutes.

MAIN CHAKRA HEALING COLOURS:
All the rainbow colours.

PURPOSE

CARD MEANING: *Every soul that enters the earth plane has a mission to find their own true meaning in life!*

Through reincarnation and rebirth, every human being has made an agreement with their highest selves to carry out a duty or a role to master certain lessons that entail working through karmic debt and other challenges for soul growth.

As a soul progresses from one life to the next, a constant re-evaluation takes place to reduce any karma. The planet earth is a school for higher learning to work with one's gifts, talents and ideas. We all have a mission, a purpose and certain goals to achieve in every lifetime. We are all students of 'the light' that after death begins a new soul journey. Everything in life is preordained, a divine law where every soul has a destiny and a destination.

If we choose to ignore the lessons that come in life, we begin to impede our own evolutionary process on the earth. In the next incarnation, these same lessons will have to be worked through and confronted in order for the soul to move onto the next awaiting journey.

Any lessons for an individual cannot be erased, as this is impossible – we must continue to master the journey of life for spiritual wholeness and enlightenment!

AFFIRMATION: 'My soul is the inner truth that supports my desires to find my purpose in life!'

MEDITATION: Visualise the figure 8 – 'as above, so below' – which is heaven and earth. Through meditation we can connect to these two worlds together as one. Ask for divine guidance and go within to find your soul purpose and the meaning of your life path.

MAIN CHAKRA HEALING COLOURS:
Green and blue.

REFLECTION

CARD MEANING: *Enter your mind into a zone of peace by working with meditation to still the mind.*

You can train the mind to become clear and focused. Too many thoughts can create confusion. If the mind behaves like a monkey, with too much clutter and constant internal chatter, we may end up having a mental breakdown! The brain is like a computer; it has the ability to store information, to process logic, to analyse, record memory, rationalise thoughts and retain visual images!

As human beings we only use a small percentage of the brain. We have a lot more potential to work with this intricate organ by learning various techniques with mental exercises for discipline.

Meditation is great for concentration, memory and helpful for clarity! At any time, when we have to make some important decisions in life it is advisable to reflect on the issue first! Don't rush into anything, think it out loudly and write it down. This will help not to overlook anything, to become clear about the situation and will help for guidance.

At times we often need to confront certain experiences, to find the right path of action! Every one of us that has come into this world has been given the power of free will. It is up to the individual how she or he uses it!

AFFIRMATION: 'The time has come to reflect within my soul to find the right path of action. I trust and respect my decision!'

MEDITATION: Find a tranquil place to meditate and to relax the mind. Focus on the word 'reflection' to bring in harmony and peace for the heart. Visualise the art work image on page 63 (Crown Chakra Geometry Map), to transcend your mind to another zone of spiritual consciousness, leaving behind the busy world of chatter!

MAIN CHAKRA HEALING COLOURS:
Green and blue.

RELAXATION

CARD MEANING: *The body is the temple for our soul, we must learn to take some time out to re-energise, to de-stress and to nurture our inner being!*

Take some time out to relax the mind. The best and easiest way to get re-vitalised is to spend some time with nature. All work and no play does not help to achieve balance for one's own life! During times of stress or having a busy work schedule, we can put a lot of pressure and tension into our own body. Be careful of reaching a state of burn out; feeling exhausted, tired and moody can bring on depression.

Don't feel guilty; take some time out to unwind! Book a holiday, go on a trip or find a health spa to get pampered! There are many ways of re-charging your body; the simplest one is to connect with the earth by walking with your bare feet on the grass, soil, beach, garden or anywhere that has natural surroundings.

Enjoy the gift of Mother Nature in all of her glory that contains healing powers from the earth. Sense the smells and fragrances of the many living flowers and other plants that are found nearby. Listen to the calls of nature like the birds singing, the bees humming, the wind in the trees, and the crash of the sea waves. It is all around us, like the striking colours of the sunsets that are found in the skies! Spend some time relaxing near the sea or a place that is near the water; this is conducive for healing. The element of water represents tranquillity, calmness and serenity!

Learn to embrace the beautiful energy from the sun. These powerful solar rays can help to re-vitalise the body and to bring in upliftment for the soul! A dose of natural sunlight for at least thirty minutes is a good source of vitamin D for the bones.

AFFIRMATION: 'I make the time to have relaxation in my life! I feel good!'

MEDITATION: Visualise a place of peace and let your mind drift to that zone of consciousness. Use your imagination to create these surroundings; smell the air, feel the colour and the tranquillity that it brings. Stay in the moment for at least fifteen minutes.

MAIN CHAKRA HEALING COLOUR:
Green and violet.

ROMANCE

CARD MEANING: *A feeling of passion and excitement with someone that is close to your heart on an intimate level!*

Plan a candlelit dinner, go out to a lovely restaurant, visit the theatre; be creative to follow your heart's desire with that someone special that is in your life! If you are single, expect a new romance that could end up as a loving, giving and nurturing relationship!

To find love, we have to keep our own heart open! Are you ready to receive the same energy in return for a serious commitment? If you are already in a long term relationship, expect a renewal of love and a further deepening of feelings for each other. Show and express to your partner how you really feel about them! Surprise them with a gift of chocolates, flowers, perfume or something that is personal and fun!

When we feel good about ourselves, we draw in love like a magnet. The universe contains healing light, love and many blessings for everyone to have. We can channel this powerful energy from above to give something back also to the earth for healing.

AFFIRMATION: 'I dance along the merry path of finding true love, happiness and bliss!'

MEDITATION: Visualise the colour red for passion, vitality, sexuality and romance. Work with the colour green for healing the heart and magenta for unconditional love from the angelic realm.

MAIN CHAKRA HEALING COLOURS:
Red, green and magenta.

SACRED SITE

CARD MEANING: *The Earth has been endowed with powerful spiritual and natural landscapes that are found all around the world. Some have been built by our ancient ancestors that accessed the mysteries of life. Each holy place can contain healing energy for rejuvenation, cleansing, upliftment of the soul and clearing of negative energies.*

You may be urged to follow a 'spiritual calling' to a destination that has a purpose for your soul. Sometimes this can be a strong feeling that we have to follow; a sense of being overwhelmed that has to be followed with faith and trust. This can be in any form; a new business location, a connection to someone, karmic return about a location in the past that needs to be healed, to find an answer, an unresolved mystery, the body to become re-energised, to become aware about an idea, etc. We need to listen to our intuition and realise that sometimes we are not in control; but look at these experiences as an adventure all the same! Become a seeker and you shall find the reason that is behind your task.

Nothing comes by chance; we are all interconnected to mind fields of energy where distance has no boundaries. By visiting a sacred site, whether it is a holy temple, a natural spring, an Aztec pyramid, the top of a mountain, a sea pool, sitting under a beautiful old tree etc. we can absorb the environmental energy that offers peace, serenity and healing for the mind.

AFFIRMATION: 'I am in a beautiful place of nature to be respected, and I thank the divine for sharing this gift for all of us to share.'

MEDITATION: Find a place that gives you inspiration; it can be an outside location or somewhere inside. Sit and relax, focus on the mind and sense the surrounding environment. Feel its energy, breathe in the air to fill your lungs and breathe out slowly. Repeat this several times. Also note any smell that may linger in the air. Visualise in your third eye a colour that may come to you without any thought. If you receive a colour, direct it to the specific Chakra in the body that needs re-energising.

MAIN CHAKRA HEALING COLOURS:
All the rainbow colours.

SOLAR PLEXUS GEOMETRY MAP

CARD MEANING: *The Chakra centre that represents one's own spiritual power for being assertive, deals with inner authority, acknowledgement and study. This energy centre also connects with our self-worth, our own self-esteem, confidence, the intellect, happiness and for joy!*

The location of this Chakra is between the upper bowels and the heart. The organs which function with this Chakra are the stomach, liver and the digestive system. The Chakra connects directly with the nervous system and the skin.

If this chakra becomes stressed, blocked or overloaded, the imbalance can create a level of dis-easement in this area. Any form of illness can be due to one's own mental state, like not feeling good about oneself, too much negative thinking, doubt about one's own abilities, being unhappy, having selfish motives, any kind of fears which can create complex phobias, anxieties or any other mental disorders.

Any negative emotion can affect our own inner wellbeing for harmony, peace and balance. Try to stay positive, be optimistic and have happy thoughts! The Solar Plexus Chakra is yellow in colour. Bright colours have good high chi energy for upliftment and joy!

AFFIRMATION: 'I honour my true self-worth and think of happy thoughts for success and inner wellbeing!'

MEDITATION: Visualise the Solar Plexus Geometry Map as illustrated on page 149. The colour yellow of the sun is radiant and powerful for healing.

MAIN CHAKRA HEALING COLOUR:
Yellow.

SOLITUDE

CARD MEANING: *Enter into the zone of silence and tranquillity to find your inner soul!*

To become silent within is a powerful journey to get to know thyself! The best way to explore this spiritual pathway is to work with a simple meditation exercise. Don't be afraid of solitude, as this is a place where we get to see ourselves as we truly are! This inner mirror reflection exercise is a wonderful experience, to sense and to feel the vibration of your soul!

We are never alone in this world; we are part of nature, spirit and the cosmos. Listen to this inner zone of eternity, such as the stars and other galaxies that are found within the universal heavens! When we get to know who we really are it is possible to focus on our desires. The law of attraction has to resonate with the same vibration that is found within the soul. With joy, light and being positive, we are able to draw upon success in many different ways. Take some time out to relax and to enjoy nature! Mother Earth is a wonderful place for discovery and for self-awareness!

AFFIRMATION: 'My soul welcomes a place of peace and serenity.'

MEDITATION: Find a quiet place; it could be anywhere, on a beach, in a park, by the river or at home. Sit and go into the meditation exercise. Go deep within to connect to your soul, listen to the stillness and feel at one with the cosmos.

MAIN CHAKRA HEALING COLOUR:
Orange.

SOUL GROWTH

CARD MEANING: *Mankind is a 'light vessel'; within the body there is a soul. We have all come to the earth world to learn and to grow.*

Before a soul re-enters the earth plane, it must choose its origin of birth and its parents. This karmic link that is with others has a spiritual connection and a path of destiny. The soul must work through lessons and karmic patterns for soul growth! Every life for a soul has been mapped out by the Creator. The divine supports our lessons and we are here to challenge ourselves and to learn about the two worlds that we all share. Above is heaven, and below is earth. Life is a mystery and if you would like to explore other different worlds, it is worth while reading about philosophy, mysticism, theosophy and ancient knowledge.

In the area of philosophy from Buddhism, the teachings of this doctrine relates to karma and reincarnation. A soul is a seed of light that has entered into a physical body. It is born and reborn again from many different lifetimes. Every soul has an 'akashic record'; a history of information that contains a person's previous past life experiences. A spiritualist called an 'all-knowing clairvoyant' is able to tap into this library of information. However the first law is to ask for permission from the client that is having the consultation. The information channelled from the divine can assist someone in the area of healing with a past life condition that has been carried forward in the present life.

To know and to confront any karmic issue, is working on the soul for higher learning and for enlightenment. One's own life is already preordained, it has been written in the heavens! Let the journey begin!

AFFIRMATION: 'The lessons I receive in this lifetime are for my highest good! I am open to overcome any challenges in my life, which are blessings in disguise to assist my soul's growth!'

MEDITATION: Sit quietly and become silent within. Connect to your soul consciousness to awaken the spirit within – 'I am a flame of eternal light!'

MAIN CHAKRA HEALING COLOURS:
All the rainbow colours.

STAGNATION

CARD MEANING: *Nothing is moving forward, all things have come to a standstill!*

The situation is on hold, but try not to force things; just go with the flow! This is a waiting period; a time of transition that is taking place until the wheel of destiny turns again. Don't waste valuable time, use it wisely to get things organised, tie up any loose ends, de-clutter the home or office, work on new ideas and take some time out to rest!

Nothing in life will remain the same forever, so look forward to the next upcoming event. Try to stay positive during this temporary period and trust in the process! When a situation becomes blocked, this will test one's own patience, belief and faith. To help move things forward, work with daily meditations to visualise the desired outcome.

Release any worries or fears, stay focused and have some fun! Co-operate with the universe and heal yourself of anything that no longer has value or importance in your life. Let go and become free!

AFFIRMATION: 'The situation will improve in time. I let go of anything that has no purpose or meaning in my life!'

MEDITATION: Visualise 'The Karma Card' art image on page 93, to be one with the centre of the universe. Resonate with this painting titled 'Starburst' to enter into a zone of silence. We will need to apply patience, understanding and tolerance for others that has to be earned.

MAIN CHAKRA HEALING COLOUR:
Red.

STRENGTH

CARD MEANING: *You are about to become stronger!*

In times of facing adversity in life or experiencing troubled times we have to believe in ourselves. We must confront the challenge by honouring our truth, having faith, seeking courage and willpower to make things become better. Often we can share the strength that we have with others, by giving support, assistance, listening to their needs and just by being there for them in whatever circumstance.

We can call upon strength for healing, especially if we have lost a loved one, dealing with any crisis or an illness! The angels are our friends and guides, so call upon them at any time for help! If an injustice has been committed, we need to stand up for ourselves! We must learn to speak our truth, as this is our seat of inner power. Honesty delivers good karmic benefits for ourselves and for others!

If our body becomes weak, we have to strengthen it by exercise. Any physical activity helps to reduce stress, keeps us healthy and promotes positive thinking for the mind. Exercise is good for our body, helps to improve self-image, and raises our confidence and our self-esteem in a positive way.

AFFIRMATION: 'My strength is shown in kindness, compassion and empathy for others!'

MEDITATION: Visualise the Base Chakra Geometry Map on page 39 for strength, courage and willpower. You can also work with the Solar Plexus Chakra Geometry Map on page 149 for releasing fear, to feel positive about oneself and to bring in joy.

MAIN CHAKRA HEALING COLOURS:
Red and yellow.

SURRENDER

CARD MEANING: *Allow yourself to live in the moment, to go with the flow.*

In life we have to earn trust as this cannot be given freely to any individual. If you are in doubt, feeling negative or stuck in a karmic pattern which does not support you any more, then we need to take the necessary steps of having time out to re-evaluate the issue that is causing the block. If you would like to receive some guidance on this matter, practice the way of meditation to connect to the higher realm for intuitive insight. Be patient with this process as you will also need to be prepared for a change. This transformative process will allow you to create your desires that are aligned with your highest good. As time does not stand still, you will realise a valuable lesson to overcome which will allow yourself to become more detached and free. It is time to let go of any worries or negative thinking which is a waste of time. If you create too much stress, this alone can become detrimental to your health and inner wellbeing. Take time out to exercise as this will help to release any anxieties, any built up inner tension or any suppressed energy that the body needs to expel to feel more at peace.

Don't fight against the path of least resistance as this can only slow things further down to a grinding halt. The light angels ask of you to keep the leap of faith. Send your prayers over to the universe and relax! Don't think too much about how it will turn out, try to become detached to allow the path of destiny to work for you!

The intention or a wish may be strong to act upon, you may want to visit a sacred place for rejuvenation or offer someone help without any expectations in return or volunteer your time for a charity cause?

If you are waiting for a reply, keep busy as this will help to move things along in the flow of life!

If the pathway of a goal is aligned with your higher sole purpose, it will come to fruition.

We can be ready to achieve our goals, however waiting on others can sometimes be a patient game!

Spirit will never allow anyone to feel abandoned, alone or to be misguided.

AFFIRMATION: 'I trust in the process of life by connecting with the divine laws of life'

MEDITATION: Imagine yourself curled up on a sofa or on a bed, surrounded by a soft pink fluffy blanket of love. Feel the warmth and imagine pink roses around you with their sweet perfume filling the room. Ask the angels of the light for guidance and have faith that during this time it will bring you clarity and direction. Let go of any worries and negative thoughts that may hinder your progress.

MAIN CHAKRA HEALING COLOURS:
Violet and magenta.

THIRD EYE CHAKRA GEOMETRY MAP

CARD MEANING: *The Chakra centre that opens the doorway of third sight, vision, and ideas – it also opens the ability to see beyond to non-material things which is known as clairvoyance.*

This energy centre is indigo in colour and connects to the pineal glands that are found within the body. The third eye when activated helps to see the truth behind any situation. Be guided with your own feelings and intuition and explore the path of higher knowing.

This Chakra centre also relates to the mind; our thoughts are like energy fields which can help to manifest our desires to the outer world. The law of attraction resonates with one's own thought patterns. The challenge is to become responsible for one's own actions, words, deeds and inner thoughts. The moon vibrates with this energy centre, which opens the gateway of our highest selves, the subconscious, our own consciousness and connects to the realm of spirit.

The Third Eye Chakra can be activated to help assist visionaries, pioneers, leaders and all other creative artisans. Visionary concepts help to revolutionise the world and to help advance mankind's evolution on earth.

AFFIRMATION: 'My third eye is open and clear – I choose to see what is beyond, working with inspiration and ideas to guide my life!'

MEDITATION: Visualise the Third Eye Chakra Geometry Map to awaken the ability for third sight and for divine guidance.

MAIN CHAKRA HEALING COLOUR:
Indigo blue.

THROAT CHAKRA GEOMETRY MAP

CARD MEANING: *The Chakra centre for communication and creative expression.*

This energy centre is blue in colour and connects to the thyroid glands in the body. The symptoms of a stressed Throat Chakra can relate to sore throats, having to clear the throat or coughing before actually speaking. An underactive or overactive thyroid gland can bring in weight loss or weight gain. The immune system is connected to any imbalance that is found within the body. If a person's energy level is low, the response of the immune system can become sluggish and slow. Any type of infection or viral activity needs extra energy from the auto immune system to combat the dis-easement or illness for healing. Other health problems related to this Chakra centre can also affect the heart.

The Throat Chakra links to our verbal communication and speech. We need to speak openly about the way we feel. If we end up suppressing our way of communication through fear, anger or self-worth issues this Chakra will become affected. We need to 'walk our talk' in life; this action will help to bring in clarity, focus and self-respect for oneself. In a relationship don't be afraid to speak from your heart. This is your truth and our power centre.

Be open and spontaneous when it comes to communication! When you are being challenged by someone, think first then deliver your verbal expression in a diplomatic manner. Try some tenderness to get to the point or an idea that you would like to explain. It is important to be who you are!

AFFIRMATION: 'My communication with others is open, direct and clear!'

MEDITATION: Visualise the Throat Chakra Geometry Map. All the heavenly blue colours will help to activate healing for this centre of creative expression.

MAIN CHAKRA HEALING COLOUR:
Blue.

TIME TRAVEL

CARD MEANING: *Enter into the universe where other time dimensions exist. Open your mind to sense unexplored planets and other unknown worlds.*

Allow your mind to become adaptable and flexible to the possibility of other terrestrial life forms that can be found within the cosmos. The planet earth is rich in all life forms, with plants, animals, minerals, water, air and other natural resources that are needed for mankind's survival.

The earth is directly linked with the solar system, where the sun is the most important heavenly body; it gives us light energy, sustenance and supports all living creatures that co-habit the planet. Without the sun, nothing could survive on earth!

The guardians of the universe watch over the earth, observing mankind's role, responsibility and actions that concern the ecosystem for the living environment.

Higher beings of light may enter the earth zone to assist mankind's evolutionary plan, working in consideration with the laws of dharma, destiny and universal laws which are directly linked to the divine source that created the cosmos! As human beings we have much to learn about our own spiritual development, working with the light of knowledge and understanding the laws of the universe that operate within the existence of life.

AFFIRMATION: 'I am a part of the universe; it flows through my body, heart, spirit and my soul!'

MEDITATION: This is a powerful healing session for any illness or dis-easement that is found within the body and can be used any time.

Sit in an open space underneath the night sky. Visualise the light rays of the moon, the sun, the stars and other heavenly bodies in the cosmos. Now bring the rays of light through your Crown Chakra and move this universal energy source down to the Base Chakra.

Bathe in this beautiful healing light for at least fifteen minutes. Enjoy it and relax whilst being rejuvenated.

MAIN CHAKRA HEALING COLOURS:
All the rainbow colours.

TRANSCENDENCE

CARD MEANING: *The moment waits for mankind to step into the next evolutionary process which is connecting to a higher plane of consciousness called spiritual awareness!*

This next level of transformation has the purpose of awakening mankind's spiritual senses which will help to connect with the path of higher learning. The spiritual veil that co-exists with the earth plane is changing and becoming more accessible. This world of light and spirit wants to assist with earthly matters that will offer the human race a quicker ascension to bring in healing energy for the planet. The time of importance is now to help advance mankind's evolutionary path and for its future survival on our earth.

Mankind is part of the cosmos, in nature and in all other things that represent the earth. The universe is filled with cosmic energy, light, colour, sound, supernatural powers, gases, different time dimensions which contain other forms of terrestrial life and intelligence, the unexplored and unexplained galaxies. In the future, mankind will try to understand these complex mysteries of the universe that we all share and live in.

The main concern for living in the 21st century is to resolve the global climatic change that is occurring right now on our earth. Any temperature changes on our planet can have drastic consequences for all of life, which includes mankind. The numbers of endangered species are becoming more evident, which has been on the rise. Many animals, insects, fish, birds, mammals, amphibians, plants, etc. are becoming extinct at a rapid rate! Mankind is wiping out these species over time, one by one!

AFFIRMATION: 'By being open to universal realities, I am able to perceive and observe a higher power! My soul is light; I now see clearly who I am!'

MEDITATION: Visualise The Crown Chakra Geometry Map on page 63 to connect to a higher plane of consciousness.

MAIN CHAKRA HEALING COLOUR:
Violet.

TRANSFORMATION

CARD MEANING: *To create a change, moving from one situation to another for learning that will help to better ourselves!*

Like all cycles in nature, nothing stays the same! All things remain transient, like the caterpillar that sleeps in its cocoon, and then breaks out to become a beautiful butterfly!

Part of our journey is to accept change, whether we like it or not. Letting go of old habits and patterns that we have outgrown gives way for the new. In life we continually learn to grow through lessons and other challenges. Let go of any fears, confront the situation to heal and to move on. Spread your wings like the butterfly to find new adventures! An exciting journey is about to unfold, which will be rewarding, fun and challenging. Be brave and bold, grab this opportunity – it is for you to take right now!

If you have been in a rut, try something new to revitalise your soul! Take the risk, take the leap of faith and go with the flow. This transformative process is another natural cycle to work with and to trust. A soul is reborn again and again, to find its destination of eternal bliss and happiness!

AFFIRMATION: 'I embrace the new journey that awaits my soul! I am free to accept this challenge – I let go of the past that has no more meaning or purpose! Amen.'

MEDITATION: Visualise the beautiful painting called 'The Butterfly Dance', and feel the freedom and the joy! Spread your wings to the song and the magic of this nature world that we all share.

MAIN CHAKRA HEALING COLOURS:
Yellow and violet.

TRUST

CARD MEANING: *To walk the path of truth, to install faith that everything will turn out the way it should – according to the law of karma.*

Life is going to have many challenges that will test our patience, the belief within ourselves and the focus to achieve a desired result. Stay persistent and remain dedicated to the task! Release any worries, doubt or conflicts over to the angels. Rest assured in their support, strength, comfort and joy. As you begin to learn the process of trust, this will only empower you to know that everything is going to be alright!

Most things in life are all preordained; no use fighting it as this will become a waste of time. There is an old saying, 'what resists actually persists!' We can only learn and grow by our mistakes. It is only through certain experiences that we will get to attain wisdom to create success.

Every life lesson is a blessing to make us become more aware and not to take things for granted.

Allow yourself to be guided by your highest self and go by your intuition. Trust those feelings that we receive from the unseen world; the next concern is not to rationalise or analyse it with your mind. We will end up in a state of confusion which unfortunately will show that we have missed the whole meaning and purpose to it!

AFFIRMATION: 'I learn to trust in the process of life, in order to learn and to grow!'

MEDITATION: Visualise the Third Eye Chakra Geometry Map on page 161 to open the gateway of the angelic realm for higher guidance to receive psychic cognition, perception and working with one's own ideas for direction.

MAIN CHAKRA HEALING COLOUR:
Indigo blue.

UNIVERSE

CARD MEANING: *Enter into the cosmos that is filled with colour, light, sparkling stars, planets, galaxies and other new worlds to be found!*

The universe has no starting point and no ending! It is a time zone of the unknown that contains supernatural forces, complex time dimensions and other forms of terrestrial life. The universe is within us and resonates outside of us! We as human beings have originated from this seed of light that has been created by a higher power.

The earth, which is the richest in minerals and resources of all other planets, is the home base for the galaxy enterprise.

In ancient times, the Egyptians who built the pyramids were a superior race beyond time and space! These so called 'cosmic architects' were known also as 'alchemists' who knew the laws of quantum physics, astrology and metaphysics. They were also powerful healers that worked with herbs, natural gemstones, crystals and light for healing.

The Egyptian pyramids were built under a star navigational system that created an open doorway for time travel and for communication to the heavens. The top part of the pyramid chamber was used for meditation and for healing. This position was closest to the universal energy stream which was used for healing and channelling in light vibration. Other ancient civilisations that roamed the earth have left a powerful imprint for mankind to try to understand and to evaluate about other mysteries of life.

AFFIRMATION: 'I hold the universe in my soul; it is within my grasp to understand and to explore!'

MEDITATION: Find a quiet place, sit and become still. The next step is to visualise the stars, the sun and other cosmic bodies of the universe. Bring these beautiful light rays of colour into your body to re-energise, heal and uplift your inner being.

MAIN CHAKRA HEALING COLOURS:
All the rainbow colours.

WHOLENESS

CARD MEANING: *To feel content within, to have inner peace, harmony, wellbeing and happiness!*

When our lives become too stressful, we need to take a step backward to re-evaluate our actions.

Karmically, we should be in the centre of the wheel of life; being in control and flowing with the law of balance. This is how we can maintain good health, longevity and mental clarity. We have to remind ourselves that in order to achieve balance, it does take effort, awareness and discipline. The body is our temple for the soul; we need to eat healthy foods, drink plenty of fresh water, regularly exercise, spend some time outdoors for at least thirty minutes of natural sunlight and take some time out to relax including meditation. It is possible to integrate these activities in our daily life with a dose of positive thinking.

At any time giving something back to the community or caring for our beautiful Mother Earth helps to create wholeness which leads to happiness. When we feel out of balance or disconnected with the flow of life, it is time to work on this balance again to bring everything back to its perspective.

AFFIRMATION: 'I commit myself to obey the rules of living in harmony with Mother Nature!'

MEDITATION: An easy technique to help still the mind is to visualise a place of peace. Close your eyes and imagine a beautiful place that you would love to be in. Centre your being with the grounding technique on page 199. Get into this zone for at least fifteen minutes to reflect and to release any stress or worries to bring in harmony for the mind, body and spirit.

MAIN CHAKRA HEALING COLOURS:
All the rainbow colours.

WISDOM

CARD MEANING: *To attain great knowledge, a path of higher learning by experiencing life lessons and the challenges that comes with them!*

The ability to use discrimination, discernment, logic and common sense which helps to guide one's own life. Wisdom resonates on a level of heightened perception which helps to achieve goals, to resolve any situation and to analyse any delusions or hidden agendas from others with perfect clarity.

When making decisions, take your time to find the path of balance. Follow your heart centre which is your power and your truth! Be guided by the way you really feel, followed by honesty and listening to your highest self. Wisdom can be used to overcome any situation by maintaining the right action to bring in order, liberation and for any kind of resolution.

Take some time out to read and to learn about philosophy, philanthropy, Tao, Buddhism and Zen which all connect to the laws of universal wisdom. To become a wise person takes time; you will need to master every lesson that life has to offer. Every being on earth has this challenge to conquer. Actions and words create a karmic force of return, the same energy will be sent back to the owner, so become careful and aware of your thoughts!

AFFIRMATION: 'My life is in the flow, and I listen to my inner voice for wisdom and guidance!'

MEDITATION: Visualise the art image of 'Water Lilies' on page 105. Ask the Buddha, gods and goddesses for any insight, for help, support and to give wisdom! Work with grace for humility, compassion and ask for forgiveness if need be for peace and integration.

MAIN CHAKRA HEALING COLOUR:
Orange.

WISHES

CARD MEANING: *Think about what you truly desire and ask for it to be given!*

If it is something that you truly deserve, it will come your way. To make it happen, we can believe in 'magic' by working with the power of positive thought!

Remember any wish must remain a secret, otherwise it will become broken! The magical kingdom is found within Mother Nature. Use your inner eye to imagine and to visualise the fairies, elves, leprechauns and other enchanted beings that play in this world! The fairies have special powers to help relationship issues, to bring in healing, happiness, joy, upliftment and fun! The Deva kingdom of nature can also represent the angelic realm. Their work is to help heal the earth, to bring in harmony and to offer environmental awareness on a global level.

Nature is precious and fragile. Take some time to give something back to Mother Earth. Why not plant a tree, create a garden, water the flowers, make compost or anything else to nurture our living environment? Most importantly, send some kind and loving thoughts to our precious earth. The angels have another task – to look after the animal and plant kingdom. Go visit a zoo, an animal park or make a donation to any nature fund.

AFFIRMATION: 'To wish is a magical process for belief and a blessing for good work done!'

MEDITATION: Think of magic! Visualise the 'power luck symbol' of the Angelic Guidance Geometry Map which is the eighth energy vortex sitting above the head (see page 35).

MAIN CHAKRA HEALING COLOURS:
All the rainbow colours.

CHAPTER SIX

THE AURIC COLOUR FIELD OF THE BODY CHAKRAS

As illustrated in the diagram on page 10, every Chakra positioned in the body has an energy field that has a specific colour code. These colours extend from the Chakra to the outer body zone. These subtle energy colour flows cannot be seen by the naked eye. If you were to sense these colours, you would see them like the rainbow. The high vibration of these colours are truly amazing and so beautiful! By awakening the Third Eye Chakra, it is possible to see them physically or view the colour within your mind.

The field of the body aura will change most of the time; like a chameleon lizard that adapts to the colour of its living environment for survival, we are also similarly on a daily basis affected by our moods and emotions.

If we are feeling happy and at peace, the colours of our outer body auric field will become more predominant with the colours of green and yellow.

A person who is very much in love will have pink and red for passion in their aura.

A mystic healer will have more violet and indigo blue in their auric field. The violet connects to the psychic realm and indigo blue brings in clairvoyance and visionary ideas.

A creative writer may have turquoise and blue for media communication in their aura.

It is most likely that every human being will be drawn to a particular colour for the day depending on their mood and how they feel.

For example, a person that wears the colour blue for the day may represent their career in communication with people. The colour blue denotes the Throat Chakra to give it more support and energy thus keeping this centre more open and flowing.

If a person decides to wear red for the day, it can indicate that their energy levels are low, feeling exhausted and tired. The colour red helps to bring in more energy for motivation and to combat lethargy! It is an energising colour for vitality.

If a person wears a lot of yellow most of the time, on a subconscious level they are drawn to this colour vibration to heal the stomach area, which resonates with the Solar Plexus Chakra. It also can be an emotional issue where the person suffers anxiety, fear, may have self-worth issues or worries too much to create stress in this particular zone of the body.

The mind is ruled by our subconsciousness which we automatically connect without knowing. The body gives signals and warnings when something is not balanced in regard towards our own healthy constitution. It is often that we do not listen to our own body, as our focus and awareness is attuned to the outer living environment. Some people choose not to be connected to their body, rather living in their own head. When the body mechanism becomes weak or not in balance, the physical body becomes sick to tell us that we have to take notice of a certain problem.

We have to treat any form of illness holistically, which also connects our state of mind, our emotions, our mental, spiritual, and then physical states.

Most illnesses start from the outside of the aura and then it work their way lastly into the physical body which can affect the Chakras.

If these energy Chakras become blocked, illness could prevail where one may feel sluggish and tired. The chi level for these centres will be low in energy. By introducing colour therapy for the body, one may unblock and thus assist with increasing the vibrational flow within that particular Chakra. When these wheels of energy are naturally free flowing, we begin to heal, to open and re-energise the body for harmony and balance.

COLOUR AREAS OF THE BODY

Red:	From the feet to the waist.
Orange:	Lower portion of the intestines and the lower back.
Yellow:	Navel and sacral area.
Green:	Heart and upper thoracic area of the back.
Turquoise:	Collar bone and the shoulders.
Blue:	Throat, lower jaw and cervical area of the neck.
Indigo Blue:	Forehead and the back of the head.
Violet:	The top of the head and temples.
Magenta:	Above the head are the angelic realm, intuition and divine guidance.

CHAPTER SEVEN

HOW DOES COLOUR HEALING WORK?

The human body and all living things have an 'aura'. This energy field extends outside the body and radiates outwardly. The aura contains many different colours depending on one's mood, emotions and personality of the soul. This energy field will tend to change according to what a person may be experiencing in life at the time. If a person becomes angry, the aura field will contain a lot of red. The colour red symbolises frustration, anger, passion, vitality and willpower.

Other colours can represent different meanings; for example the colour yellow is for upliftment, joy, wisdom and connects to the intellect of a person's mind. Yellow is related to the sun; its energy source makes us feel warm, happy and revitalised! By introducing the colour of yellow to the body, this can help to improve one's chi energy, especially if someone is suffering from anxiety, fear, depression or sadness.

The body's organs vibrate to a specific energy field. These bands relate to certain colours as illustrated in the diagram on page 183.

HOW DOES COLOUR HEALING WORK FOR THE BODY?

It is useful to study colour theory to know what colours are used for healing the Chakras that are found within the body. Knowledge is vital information for any form of self-help healing! Once colour is implemented properly by working with the Colour Medicine Oracle Cards, understanding the colours as outlined in chapter three, and the meditation and visualisation techniques on page 196, one can create balance and harmony for the body, mind, and the soul.

If any one of these energy centres that are called Chakras become blocked, stressed or overloaded, a certain level of illness can prevail or dis-easement can be found within the body. When the body energy system stagnates within its own energy flow, one may feel exhausted, which can create laziness because there is simply a lack of energy.

The universal energy system in life is called chi which is also found within the human body. An abundant supply of chi energy flow for the body helps to maintain good health and inner wellbeing. The Chakras need to be always in harmony to achieve balance for one's own body health system.

The Chakra Angel

CHAPTER EIGHT

POSITIVE AFFIRMATIONS FOR HEALING

Every oracle card connects with a subject theme which relates to a Chakra or Chakras that connect on an emotional, mental, spiritual and physical level of mankind. The use of affirmations helps to create positive responses and suggestions for motivation and to connect with the divine power for self-help healing.

By confronting and understanding a life challenge or by knowing the lesson, you can take action to resolve a situation, which is a big task for everyone to master! The purpose of life is for soul growth; to learn through many lessons and experiences from the world we all live in.

Any Chakra blockage created by a negative emotion such as stress can be confronted and released by working with a positive affirmation. This will help to achieve a level of higher awareness on the mental and spiritual plane of the person's belief system. By working with the affirmation, this will offer support, balance and harmony within the Chakra that has to be healed.

Most importantly it will help to stabilise the energy centre, to gain a sense of inner peace followed by happiness and joy! Through wisdom and guidance, this can be achieved to choose the best possible path for direction, giving insight on how to deal with any given situation for our own highest good. Most problems can be resolved through positive action.

CHAPTER NINE

HOW TO USE THE ORACLE CARDS

THE COLOUR MEDICINE ORACLE CARD DECK LAYOUTS

The Rainbow spread – Focus on a question

Think about the situation, the challenge or the subject that you would like to gain more insight for advice, and spiritual guidance that will help for direction.

This could relate to any specific area of your life, for example a relationship issue, finding a partner, working on yourself for happiness and wholeness, a health assessment, a business forecast etc.

The oracle card deck will help to clarify a situation and to offer a solution to work through any life challenge. The divine laws of karma, the art of manifestation and the lesson to learn for soul growth will assist the subject matter that is in question.

Shuffle the cards and concentrate on the question, then fan them out on a flat surface like a curved rainbow. Pick out seven cards, using your left hand for feeling and intuition. Place them in order from the first card to the last card.

Card no 1: The Past
Actions that have been taken in the past;
are they positive or negative?

Card no 2: The Present
The situation from the past has been taken into the next phase.
What influences are working through the present moment?

Card no 3: The Hidden
Unforeseen influences that could surprise or
bring in new clarity to a situation.

Card no 4: The Obstacles
What issues do we have to work through or to overcome? What
is the challenge to deal with to create a best possible outcome?

Card no 5: The environment and attitudes of other people
The chosen card will reveal a negative or a positive influence
depending on the topic behind the subject theme.

Card no 6: The advice or solution given
This will help to overcome the situation.
A practical suggestion to benefit the desired result.

Card no 7: The outcome
Advice on what can be achieved by following card 6.

The Lucky Clover Spread

Shuffle the cards then lay them out on the table like a fan. Concentrate on the question and then select four cards.

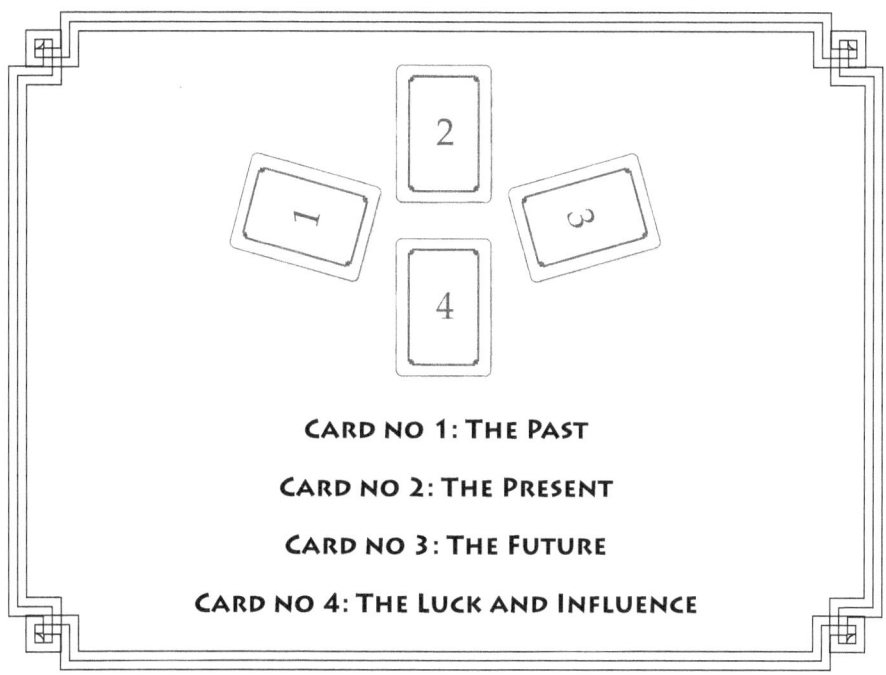

Card no 1: The Past

Card no 2: The Present

Card no 3: The Future

Card no 4: The Luck and Influence

The Angel Card Reading For Direction and Guidance

Shuffle the cards and fan them out on the table. Think about the question in your mind.

The Health Spread connecting to the Chakra system

This layout is simple to use and is designed to reveal how the Chakras are functioning in the body.

Every oracle card selected will introduce a subject theme which correlates to the Chakras that are found within the body. The advice given will include the colours required for self-help healing to bring in balance and to harmonise the energy centres.

Read the guidelines that are given for every oracle card that has been written in the book, which will introduce a colour visualisation technique for meditation and a positive affirmation for healing. The oracle cards can be used as a tool to diagnose any area of conflict or any other challenges that need to be healed in one's own life.

Any illness, imbalance or disharmony of health can be revealed by working with the oracle card deck, which will offer to assist mental clarity and self-awareness of the probable cause that created the condition.

The message will outline the current belief system of the person that is analysing the health condition of the body. One can also refer to the oracle card deck to diagnose any future and unforeseen health issues. Illness begins from the outer energy field of the body that is called the auric field which then works its way slowly into the physical body to manifest as a dis-easement.

Every oracle card has a colour Chakra bar code system which correlates to the eight Chakras which are explained in the book (see pages 12 and 195).

The colour Chakra bar code system helps to analyse the energy flow of every Chakra that is found within the body.

For example, if an oracle card has been selected for analysing the Solar Plexus Chakra and in the colour Chakra bar code is found the foundation colour of yellow, then this Chakra is balanced.

If the nominated card indicates no yellow in the colour Chakra bar code system, then this Chakra is out of balance. If the selected card has the full rainbow Chakra bar code system, then this is a good sign that the Chakra is stable and open.

Balance is the key word to maintain good health. The mind controls the body and as such any negative thinking contributes to an illness. Analysing the psychological aspects of our inner wellbeing, which includes the mental plane, the spiritual plane, and the emotional plane, we can understand how these areas can contribute towards an illness. Refer to page 12 for the spiritual psyche of colour for mankind.

For example, if one is suffering from depression, it is important to understand the past that led to the present condition. This type of illness is quite complex, referring to the belief system of the person whether holding onto negative thought processes, sadness, being pessimistic in life, evaluation of self-worth and low self-esteem, environmental factors, family history, past situation of life, outside conditioning and influences, addictions etc.

Over time, the pattern of thinking can affect the Chakras in the body to create an imbalance, thus resulting in some form of dis-easement in the body. The manifestation of any illness relates to something that has gone astray or wrong thinking on a mental level where the spiritual self is in denial with the physical body.

It is important to understand a variety of psychological issues which can relate to a specific illness.

Chakras are connected to the energy system of the body and over a period of time, one can actually create stress, blockages and imbalances within these energy centres. Factors that contribute to sickness are due to a number of psychological conditions.

One of them is being discontent in life. When we are not happy within ourselves, this does have a negative influence on our own life. Over time any negative thought patterns like fear, jealousy, bitterness, no self-love for oneself etc. can create a negative impact within our own inner being.

Another outcome of feeling isolated, unloved, low self-esteem, no confidence, confusion etc. can move a person into a 'victim role'. When one has distrust, low self-worth or feeling insecure, these conditions also contribute to becoming unwell.

The key for getting the most out of life and longevity is to have good health! Maintain balance in every area which includes getting good healthy food, fresh water, a daily dose of sunlight for thirty minutes, exercise, being positive, meditation for relaxation/stress and energy, which makes for a happy existence!

The body is our temple; we should really look after it. The intake of high fatty foods can create high blood cholesterol, arterial problems, diabetes, heart conditions, obesity, tiredness, a fatty liver and toxic waste which in turn creates dis-easement in the body!

The human body needs vitamin D which we receive for free from the sun! A daily dose of sunlight every day is essential to keep the bones and body healthy. Natural sunlight helps to alleviate depression.

Through meditation and visualising the rainbow light moving from the top of the head through the Crown Chakra and moving the energy down to the Base Chakra will help to keep the Chakras open and balanced.

Health Assessment Chakra Layout

Concentrate on the question of one's own health and ask for the status of your current situation. Now shuffle the cards, and then fan them out onto a flat surface.

Choose eight cards from the Colour Medicine Oracle Card Deck for every Chakra starting with the first card which is the Base Chakra, then working up to every other one that is found within the body.

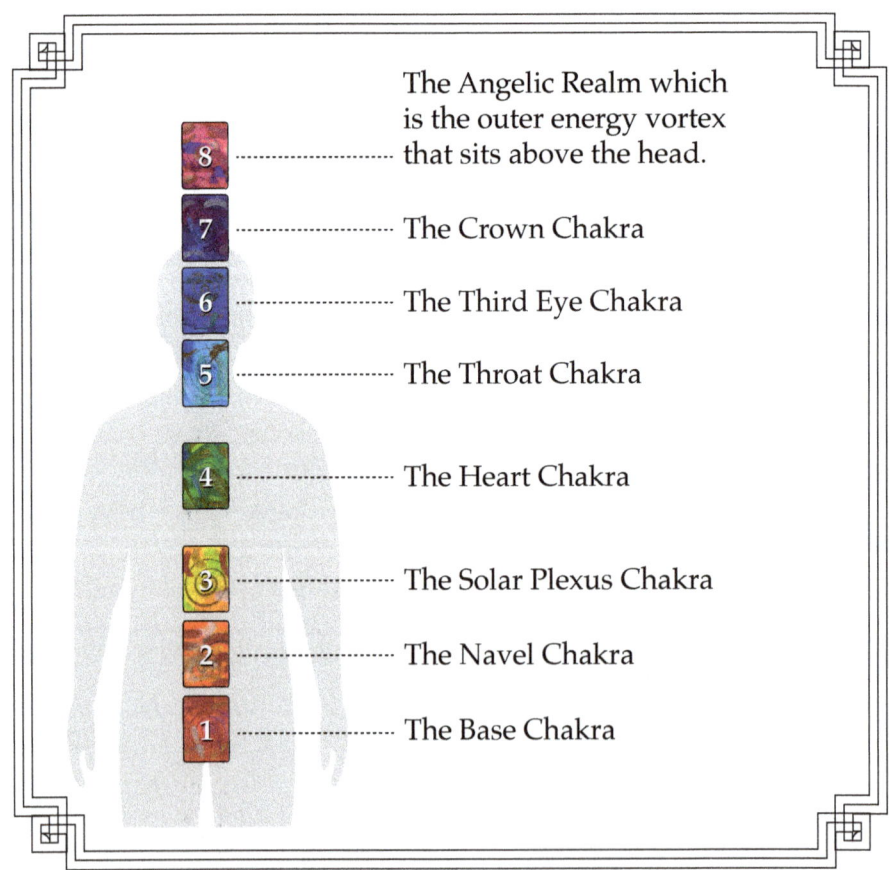

Read on the subject theme for every oracle card that has been selected and refer to 'The Spiritual Psyche of Colour for Mankind' on page 12 and 'How to Balance the Chakras' on page 135 as stated with every oracle card with the meditation technique.

An overview layout for a spiritual evaluation in one's life

This particular layout will tap into the mental, emotional, spiritual and physical plane of one's own body makeup. It will also help to evaluate and understand our highest selves.

Ask for divine guidance to observe any illness that is taking shape or form in the outer auric energy field of the body. By tapping into our highest level of consciousness, we can begin to see and understand any level of dis-easement that could occur in time.

To foresee any future illness can become preventative if action is taken to correct the way for balance. By making these corrective changes in the present, it is possible to dilute and weaken any form of dis-easement taking place from manifesting into the physical body.

By confronting psychological issues, we can begin to create a transformative process to bring in peace, harmony, good health and balance for one's own life.

Concentrate on the question of assessing one's own health. Shuffle the oracle cards and lay them out like a fan on a table.

Now pick only four cards.

CARD NO 1: THE SPIRITUAL

CARD NO 2: THE PHYSICAL

CARD NO 3: THE EMOTIONAL

CARD NO 4: THE MENTAL

CARD NO 1
The Spiritual (the aura energy field of the body): The colour for balance in this outer zone that extends from the body is violet and magenta pink. Any of these colours selected, if shown in the Chakra colour code bar system on the oracle card, represents that the outer auric energy field is strong and clear.

CARD NO 2
The Physical (the body): The colour associated for this zone is red. The colour red connects to the physical aspects of oneself for survival and represents the material plane. If the oracle card selected has the Chakra colour code bar system with the colour red, then this aspect is aligned with our body for energy flow and integrating harmony for oneself.

CARD NO 3
The Emotional (our feelings): The colour in this area is orange, a sacred colour that symbolises Buddha energy for wisdom, trust and following one's intuition. If the oracle card selected has the Chakra colour code bar system of orange, then this zone has been activated and is balanced. The colour also denotes following one's creative drive and passion in life.

CARD NO 4
The Mental (the mind): The colour in this area is yellow, as it deals with one's own thought processes that are connected to the brain. If the oracle card selected in the Chakra colour code bar system has yellow then this zone is balanced.

The colour coding message for the Oracle Card Deck
Every card selected for each Chakra will have a colour healing theme. Check the oracle cards in the book for the Chakra colour map. If the colour code is the same for the Chakra colour, then it is balanced. If the colour code does not match the Chakra colour, then it is not balanced which needs attention for healing and harmony.

As explained, if the Chakra colour is found in the bar code system on the oracle card then the Chakra is balanced. For example if you picked a card about your Heart Chakra and the card selected on the Chakra colour bar code system was found green, then this Heart Chakra is balanced. If the colour Chakra bar code system was empty, with only a white dot – then the Heart Chakra is not balanced.

If the Chakra bar code system on the selected oracle card has a vacant space with no colour, then the Chakra is not balanced.

For example, if you used the Health Assessment Chakra Layout (page 190) and chose the card COMPASSION for analysis as your Throat Chakra card, you will notice on the card's Chakra bar code system that there is no blue dot. The space is vacant with a white dot. The reading implies that the Throat Chakra is out of balance, as this area is vacant with no blue dot. The colour blue is for the Throat Chakra.

If you had selected another oracle card – TIME TRAVEL, for example – the Chakra bar code system on the card contains a blue dot. This colour code represents that the Throat Chakra is balanced.

In the last sample, if you picked the oracle card REFLECTION and questioned if your Heart Chakra was balanced, you will view on the colour Chakra bar code system there is a green and a blue dot. The Heart Chakra is green in colour, thus it is balanced.

CHAPTER TEN

HOW TO BALANCE CHAKRAS WITH ITS OPPOSITE COLOUR

To determine if a Chakra is overactive or underactive, work with meditation. Visualise every Chakra and see what comes to your mind. Colours for underactive Chakras need to be complemented with their true Chakra colour. An overactive Chakra needs to be counteracted by using the opposite colour to bring in balance.

For underactive Chakras simply use the Chakra colour chart as listed below.

Chakra	Dominant Colour	Overactive	Underactive
Base Chakra	Red	Green	Red
Navel Chakra	Orange	Blue	Orange
Solar Plexus Chakra	Yellow	Violet	Yellow
Heart Chakra	Green	Green/Pink	Green
Throat Chakra	Blue	Orange	Blue
Third Eye Chakra	Indigo Blue	Gold	Indigo Blue
Crown Chakra	Violet	Yellow	Violet

CHAPTER ELEVEN

MEDITATION AND VISUALISATION TECHNIQUES FOR HEALING

Each oracle card will relate to an artwork image that can be used to introduce a level of colour therapy for self-help healing. Every card has been designed to use as a divination tool for healing.

By using the technique of visualisation and meditation, we are able to apply a high level of healing to the body Chakras.

Sit in a quiet place where you are able to focus on your own energy without any distractions. Take a few deep breaths to calm and relax the body. Concentrate on the breathing – in and out. Before every meditation, we can use a form of psychic protection and a grounding technique (see page 200).

When one enters into a zone of consciousness we are open to explore the astral world. The first rule for connecting into the unknown is to ask for safety. Every soul has a spirit guide that can help us. It is essential to work with some form of control so that no harmful or negative energy may interfere with the meditation exercise. The second step is the term called 'grounding' which will help to connect to the higher planes of consciousness and light whilst anchored on the earth.

Begin to visualise the selected art work image of the oracle card deck and observe the colours and the shape particularly if it is a geometry Chakra map.

It is best to meditate with the eyes closed for concentration and then visualise the colour whilst absorbing its healing rays.

Breathe in the colour and feel the colour moving through your body, filling it up with its vibration and energy.

By visualising the colour flow within the mind, we can direct the specific colours to the location of the Chakras that are required for healing.

Don't stay immersed in one colour for too long; visualise for between five to eight minutes, then move on to the next Chakra colour.

Colour is absorbed directly through the eyes. Another technique is to meditate with eyes open. Observe the art image of the oracle card and direct the colours to the Chakras for healing.

As we enter into the flow of colour, it can also affect the astral field, the etheric field and the outer auric energy field. Colour is light and has a vibration which connects to one's own body energy system.

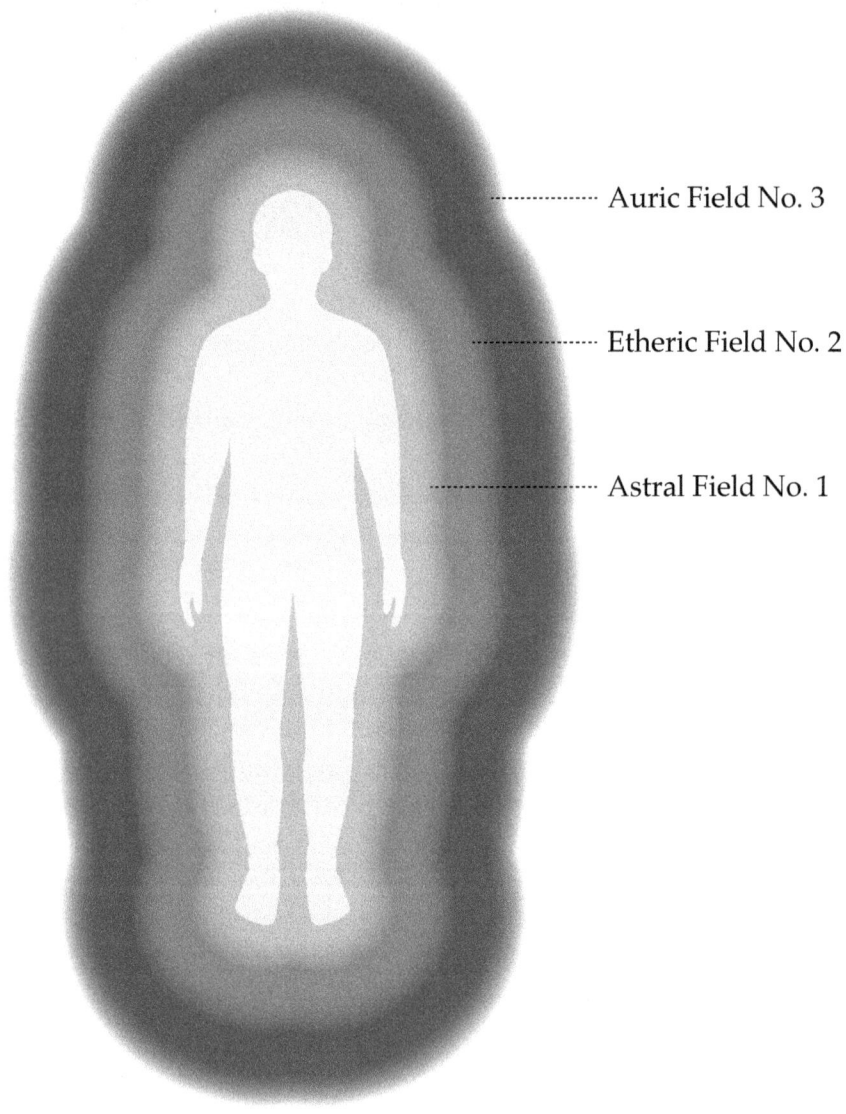

CHAPTER TWELVE

PSYCHIC PROTECTION AND GROUNDING TECHNIQUES

The first rule of thumb when entering into a state of consciousness and moving into the unknown world of spirit and light – whether performing psychic work, healing, channelling, mediumship, meditation or connecting to our loved ones – is we must ask for protection.

Before meditation, make a prayer from any religious belief that finds your true connection in life or a mantra.

The next step is to call upon the angelic realm and ask for protection. Anyone can call upon Archangel Michael, who represents a powerful guardian that can offer courage, strength and protection.

The reason to activate this force field of protection has a purpose. The most important is to assure safety and to be in control when entering into the unknown. The astral world, which is closest to the earth in spirit, does contain earth-bound entities, lost souls, the supernatural and other living systems which are not from this material plane.

There can be a danger of psychically being attacked by any entity that seeks to create havoc, harm or is just wants attention!

By activating a level of protection, this will enable us to become more focused without any distractions connecting to a higher source of energy rather than a lower base energy that filters into the lower astral world.

The third step is to visualise a bright white light like a candle flame and immerse your entire being into beautiful high energy. Sit comfortably in this bubble of beautiful white light to sense and feel the warmth, purity and radiation of intense energy.

Working with this visualisation technique of bringing in the white light around our body this will help to activate a higher vibration that can connect to higher plane of consciousness.

The fourth step is called the grounding technique. Visualise a cord of white light extending from the Navel Chakra falling down into the centre of the earth. This will help us to anchor the body, whilst connecting to the universal energy flow. We can now channel this healing source of energy through to our body.

The exercise of using meditation is a relaxed and a conscious state of being. Find a quiet place away from any distractions or noise. Whilst entering into a meditative state of consciousness, it is best to sit upright. If the body lies down flat, the mind is programmed to fall asleep.

The psychic protection technique can be used at any time when surrounded by crowds of individuals, dealing with difficult people, at work, shopping centres, on the train, bus or in any open public area.

The psychic protection energy field will help to reflect any negative energy away from the body which will help to maintain balance and inner harmony.

Short steps to remember for psychic protection and grounding

1. Make a prayer or a mantra.
2. Ask for protection and call upon Archangel Michael
3. Visualise a white light around your body.
4. Send a cord of white light from your Navel Chakra into the centre of the earth.
5. Thank the Divine and your spiritual guardians for this exercise. Amen.

CHAPTER THIRTEEN

A SPIRITUAL MESSAGE FROM THE ARTIST

It has been an interesting journey for the artist/psychic over the years to create the Colour Medicine Oracle Card Deck!

The creator of the oracle deck, Sylvia Meissner connects to the magical healing powers of colour that is found within nature. Her passion is painting nature and the purpose behind her work is to share an environmental message to the world.

The artist has worked with World Wide Fund for Nature and other global organisations that promote preservation, conservation of the environment and protection/survival of endangered species on Earth.

Her first name, Sylvia, means 'forest elf' in Latin. The artist believes that her mission is to work alongside the Deva kingdom to bring in an awareness of the fragility of nature that is found within the ecosystem of life.

The condition within an ecosystem that has become polluted, damaged or destroyed has negative repercussions for the environment including its natural inhabitants. Any negative action that abuses the environment puts further strain on the ecosystem of life.

The web of life is dependent on this natural food chain for survival. If the food chain changes, this could affect all species on a global scale offering further negative implications for the wellbeing of the planet!

Mankind must learn to share the Earth with all other living inhabitants and to live in harmony with each other. Mother Earth is a living energy system, that is alive, needs nurturing and respect from mankind. Our environment is precious, and Mother Nature is warning mankind that the earth has become out of balance.

The divine laws of nature will try to correct this balance by karmic planetary action.

Today mankind is experiencing nature's warning through global climatic change.

The earth's weather patterns are becoming unpredictable associated with floods, droughts, mudslides, tsunamis, tornadoes, cyclones, earthquakes, volcanic activity, and unusual temperature changes around the globe.

The message for mankind is to respect the land and nature. Mankind has to implement balance towards his/her needs and to take responsibility for the welfare of our precious planet.

The artist sees her role as a messenger to represent Mother Nature.

The Deva kingdom found within nature enters into the realm of magical beings, like fairies, elves, goblins, gnomes, flower spirits, angels, plant guardians and other nature entities that live on earth.

This 'world of mystical magic' exists closely with the spirit world and beyond.

Nature spirits have an important role on earth to give sustenance, medicines from plant life, beauty, healing energy through colour and light for all living species in order to survive.

Be kind to our Earth, followed by respect and most importantly we all have to take responsibility for looking after our fragile environment!

The purpose of nature, created from the divine, is for mankind to enjoy the beauty of this supernatural creation of colour, form, light, smell, to feel, texture, to sense, to observe an amazing living energy network that is a part of us. Mankind needs nature for survival and for new medicines that are found from the plant and mineral kingdom – which contain powerful healing energies.

Through the artist's work, we explore a field of holistic light medicine called colour therapy for healing the mind, body and soul. In every artwork the artist has channelled in chi energy from the universe that creates a psychic colour field for healing the body.

The application of small dots of colour that is painted onto the canvas with a brush connects to a level of chi energy.

Each particular artwork has a specific colour field vibration that becomes magnetised to a person's energy field, to help healing. The colour field of light absorbed through the eyes and a person's auric energy field helps to activate and open any stressed Chakras that are found within the physical body.

The level of consciousness of a person connects automatically with the level of colour vibration that a person needs for healing. This level of colour healing works in all areas of the human psyche which includes mental, emotional, spiritual and physical wellbeing.

By introducing the essence of divine light that works with the principles of colour healing for mankind, this is also instrumental to help advance mankind's evolution on Earth.

Art Exhibition at Central Plaza One, Brisbane

Art Exhibit at The Mind, Body & Soul

CHAPTER FOURTEEN

BIOGRAPHY OF THE ARTIST

The artist Sylvia Meissner continues to work in her own business, Healing Art Design & New Age Gallery, within Australia. She has been working as a psychic, a clairvoyant, a healer and an artist for over thirty years.

Her artistic ventures started at the age of three, connecting to colour pencils and drawing on paper. In between the ages of eleven to fifteen, her great grandmother Oma Anna gave her an oil painting set with numbers in the picture. This was easy for the young budding artist but was not a challenge! She decided to paint her own pictures, drawing animals on canvas and with her own colour technique.

Between the ages of fifteen to twenty-one, other activities were more important which simply took most of her time. The art was placed on hold, but that changed on her visit overseas ... it's called divine intervention!

On one of her holidays skiing in Aspen, Colorado in America she attended a psychic fair. Her curiosity to have a reading by a psychic was certainly eye opening. She remembers the first comment by the psychic was, 'Why are you not painting?'

At the age of twenty-five, the artist was going to pursue her art at a later time in life. The psychic suggested that Sylvia should start now and not leave it for later in old age! When the artist returned from her trip back to Australia, she decided to paint and gather a collection of works over the next five years – about thirty-four pieces for her first exhibition.

Working full time as an airline hostess was demanding and fun. The art was pursued in her leisure time over these years.

The artist launched her first solo exhibition overseas in Hong Kong. In 1996, her exhibition was held at one of the tallest buildings in Asia called Central Plaza located in Wanchai on Hong Kong Island. This event was titled 'Fragility of Nature', where the artist worked closely with the World Wide Fund for Nature – HK and the Hong Kong Cancer Fund. Funds were raised for WWF and a painting was donated to the Cancer Hospice.

The following year in 1997, another art exhibition was kindly invited by the Hong Kong Exhibition and Convention centre to display the artist's work at the Pacific Rim Restaurant. The title of the event was called 'Fire, Wind and Ice', which tapped into global warming. Much of the vision and message was advanced. In a radio interview the artist was asked why was this happening and to prove it! Her comments given were, 'Mother Earth is warning the planet that it is out of balance and if mankind does not change their ways, further natural disasters will occur!'

I don't think we really need proof when it is staring at us right in our face?

Over the next following years, the artist has displayed her works in shopping centres and her own art gallery at the Queen Victoria Building in Sydney. A gallery at Marina Mirage on the Gold Coast in Queensland offered the environmental message 'to look after our precious Earth called Mother Nature!'

In 2004, she organised an art exhibition at Burj Al Arab in Dubai, the only seven star hotel in the world, at the Assawan Amphitheatre. The exhibition was held on the 18th floor of this beautifully designed hotel, built to look like a large sail boat on the water. The event launched Colour Medicine for the 21st Century.

A few years later, in 2006, the artist organised a smaller exhibition in Shanghai, China at the World's Art Expo that was held at the National Exhibition and Convention centre. The artwork explored the Chinese elements of fire, metal, earth, water and air. The theme identified with the healing powers of colour relating to Eastern philosophy. The event title was 'Colour Medicine for the 21st Century'. The exposure of high chi energy due to the bright colours found in the art works was overwhelming for the Chinese viewers. The comment given was that they had never seen so many different fluorescent colours being used in paintings. They were certainly drawn to the paintings for excitement and for healing!

The use of colour therapy in art can be applied as a powerful healing tool for the mind, body and soul.

Other than these art exhibitions, the artist was assigned to a casino in South Dakota, USA, in 2010 to 2011 for consulting in colour healing templates for interior design, colour advisory services, commissioned art works and giclee art reproductions for the suites and rooms.

Her services also envisaged ideas and themes for the casino which was considered and implemented into the interior design of the building.

In 2013, the artist attended Artexpo New York which was held at Pier 92. Her theme for her booth explained 'Colour medicine for the 21st Century' and 'Environmental awareness'. The week of the event was dictated by a cold blizzard instead of receiving spring weather. Just another sign of karmic law from Mother Nature – that extreme weather patterns are changing all over the globe. The planet is trying to cool down the temperatures to bring in more balance for our living environment.

In 2013–2014, a 'pop up shop' was held for eight months at the Wintergarden shopping centre in Brisbane, Australia, as part of the New Age Gallery which included other colour therapy products such as Aura-Soma. These coloured bottle variations of more than 111 and growing, are made from natural plant extracts and crystals which can be applied to the body for healing.

From 2015, the business moved to Adelaide Street in the Blocksidge Building located in Brisbane. After 18 months it was time to move on and a new owner purchased the New Age Gallery.

Feeling tired with the work as a psychic and a healer, it was time for a welcome break of three years, and during this period some large pieces of art works were created that have become some important masterpieces of art in her life. During this time to keep also socially interactive, she helped her partner and owner with his restaurant business located on the prime waterfront in Brisbane, in Australia.

A further three years went past, and the artist felt intuitively that it was time again to open an art gallery and a new age shop to showcase the artist's works in Australia. Being guided by spirit, she found the perfect location in Kingscliff, NSW, to open a holistic gallery that connects to 'healing through colour and nature'. The business offers a spiritual directory of varied healing modalities such as reiki, chakra balancing, psychic readings, astrology readings, numerology, channelling, wearable energies, aromatherapy, crystals, colour therapy and other new age products to help to facilitate a further spiritual awareness and learning about one's own life journey. A level of healing can take place to find; balance, peace, joy and inner wellness for the mind, body and the soul.

The business is located opposite the beach, which has good, positive, high chi energy that is surrounded by nature with sandy beaches, clean air and an amazing green aqua sea. Further down the road is a large creek that has become a popular swimming destination, as it connects to the daily tidal changes coming from the sea. I believe this seaside town is near an important Earth Chakra within the area. It is a rare find to have a beach with a northerly and a southerly aspect.

The shop has anchored the word expression of 'a light porthole' which has been activated to bring in high energy for healing from the cosmos gateway for those that are in need to willingly receive without any preconceived judgements.

In the year 2020–2021, it is important to complete the Colour Medicine Oracle Card Deck, to get it finally published and printed. The next step is going to find a global distributor that can support this project to help the evolutionary spiritual advancement of mankind moving into the Golden Age.

Trusting and working with spirit is a patient game but can be so rewarding! Follow your dreams and adventures, the challenges of life will always be with us at any time!

TECHNICAL SKILL ABOUT THE ART

It is interesting to find the self-taught artist using a technical skill called Pointillism and Divisionism of Colour in her oil paintings. This unique style of painting that uses singular dots with a brushstroke was founded by the French Impressionists in the late 18th century. The famous French artists who founded the technique called Pointillism were Georges Seurat, Paul Signac and Henry Pissaro.

The application of using many different points of colour into one area creates more brilliance, light and luminosity into the painting. The artworks are viewed in 3D and in a 4D dimension where one can see the foreground, the middle and the distance. Every artwork is alive and energetically filled with tiny points of colour which represent the chi energy of all of life.

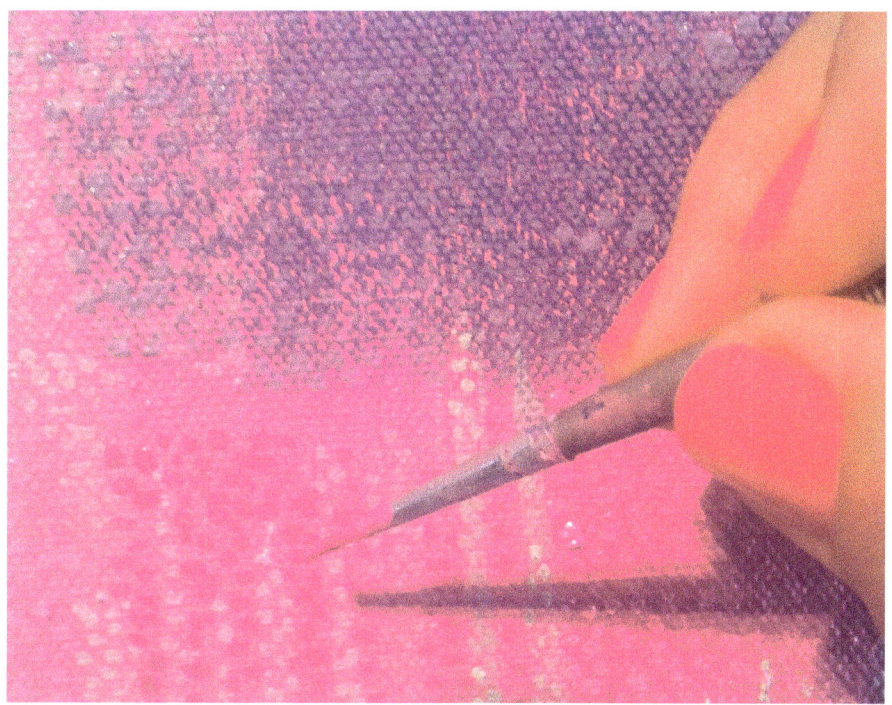

The artist's technique called 'Pointillism and Divisionism of Colour' where most paintings contain more than thousands of power point channelled dots to bring in chi energy, light, shade and movement. Connecting to colour alchemy makes these art works interesting, rare and spiritual as an energy healing painting for mankind.

As little as they knew in those older days, the French Impressionists were already combining a metaphysical skill into their work for healing! Most creative people are highly spiritual and they must have channelled the skill from a divine source without realising the full potential that it had for mankind!

CONTACT DETAILS FOR PURCHASING ART

THE COLOUR MEDICINE ORACLE DECK CARD LIST

Please note that any of these original art works and giclee reproduction art prints are available for purchase.

You may view these items on the artist's website and retail online shop at www.healingartdesign.com.au. Contact the artist by email at sylviameissner@hotmail.com or healingartdesign@outlook.com.

ORACLE CARD NAME	CHAKRA COLOUR ON BAR CODE	TITLE OF ARTWORK
1. Abundance	Red	Golden Exotic Sands
2. Acceptance	Yellow, Green and Blue	Yellow and Purple Outback Weed Carpet
3. Action	Red	Lucky Money Sea Turtle
4. Angelic Guidance Geometry Map	All Rainbow Colours	Cosmic Abundance
5. Balance	All Rainbow Colours	Infinity of Light
6. Base Chakra Geometry Map	Red	Base Chakra Geometry Map
7. Belief	Yellow	Cosmic Moon Dance
8. Bliss	Yellow	Sunflower Passion
9. Breakthrough	Red and Green	Sunset Passion
10. Celebration	All Rainbow Colours	Spiral Staircase
11. Chakra Healing	All Rainbow Colours	Rainbow Chakra Weave
12. Climate Review	Magenta	Desert Sun
13. Commitment	Yellow and Green	Barrier Reef Heart
14. Compassion	Red, Orange, Violet, Magenta and Gold	Kuan Yin Infinity of Light
15. Confusion	Red, Yellow and Violet	Lavender and Wheatfield
16. Creativity	Orange, Green and Turquoise	Paradise Desert
17. Crown Chakra Geometry Map	Violet and Magenta	Crown Chakra Geometry Map

18. Disillusion	Red, Yellow and Indigo Blue	Red Sand and Blue Sea
19. Exploration	Indigo Blue	Alternative Worlds III
20. Fertility	Red and Magenta	Rainbow Heart
21. Flexibility	Blue, Indigo Blue and Violet	Spirit Polar Bears of Aurora Borealis
22. Focus	Indigo Blue	Windsong Palms
23. Forgiveness	Green and Magenta	Cherry Blossoms
24. Freedom	All Rainbow Colours	Blue Pond I
25. Friendship	Green and Blue	Sea Horses in Play
26. Harvest	Yellow	Mt Fujiyama Blossom Magic
27. Healing	All Rainbow Colours	Bubbles of Light
28. Heart Chakra Geometry Map	Green and Magenta	Heart Chakra Geometry Map
29. Independence	Yellow	Alpine Beauty
30. Integrity	Green and Magenta	Garden of Love
31. Karma	Orange, Violet and Magenta	Starburst
32. Light Child	All Rainbow Colours	Spirit Essence
33. Loss	Yellow, Green, Violet and Magenta	Golden Sands
34. Luck	Yellow and Green	Island Dreamtime
35. Magic	All the Rainbow Colours	Elves Garden
36. Manifestation	Red, Yellow and Violet	A Field of Passion
37. Meditation	Violet	Waterlilies
38. Movement	Red, Yellow and Green	Happy Jellyfish
39. Nature	Green	Spring Harmony
40. Naval Chakra Geometry Map	Orange	Naval Chakra Geometry Map
41. Negativity	Yellow and Red	Wetland Blue
42. New Beginnings	Red and Green	Mystic Desert
43. Obsession	Green	Butterfly Dreams
44. Obstacle	Red and Blue	Star Falling
45. Partnership	Blue and Indigo Blue	Coconut Beach
46. Patience	Green, Indigo Blue and Violet	Golden Peridot Orb Stargate II
47. Persistence	Yellow	Weed Fire
48. Philosophy	Yellow and Orange	Golden Autumn Valley
49. Play	Yellow, Green and Blue	Sea Garden of Eden
50. Power	Yellow Magic	Desert Falls
51. Prayer	All Rainbow Colours	Valley of Dreams

52. Protection	Indigo Blue and White	Double Infinity of Light
53. Psychic Growth	All Rainbow Colours	Atlantis Moon Time
54. Purpose	Green and Blue	Alternative Worlds Tryptch I
55. Relaxation	Green	Water Rose's
56. Reflection	Green and Blue	Tree Reflection
57. Romance	Red, Green and Magenta	Arabic Night Sky
58. Sacred Site	All Rainbow Colours	Buddha Bodhi Tree
59. Solar Plexus Geometry Map	Yellow	Solar Plexus Geometry Map
60. Solitude	Orange	Scorched Desert
61. Soul Growth	All Rainbow Colours	Poppies
62. Stagnation	Red Alpine	Reflection
63. Strength	Red and Yellow	Buddha Hills
64. Surrender	Violet and Magenta	Pink Outback Weed Carpet
65. Third Eye Chakra Geometry Map	Indigo Blue	Third Eye Chakra Geometry Map
66. Throat Chakra Geometry Map	Blue	Throat Chakra Geometry Map
67. Time Travel	All Rainbow Colours	Alternative Worlds Trytch I
68. Transcendence	Violet	Seascape Reflection
69. Transformation	Yellow and Violet	Butterfly Dance
70. Trust	Indigo Blue	Oceania Magic
71. Universe	All Rainbow Colours	Cosmic Planets
72. Wholeness	All Rainbow Colours	Blossom Bliss
73. Wisdom	Orange	Magnetic Sunflowers
74. Wishes	All Rainbow Colours	Celestial Stardust

The beauty of nature is all within us, we are all of one from the divine source. Let us radiate and behold this beautiful energy for healing and most importantly let us save our Mother Earth for future generations to come! Amen.

The Sacred Heart Buddha Bodhi Tree of Life painting by Sylvia Meissner. >

ACKNOWLEDGEMENTS

This book is dedicated to my beautiful mother Sonja, my beloved great grandmother Oma Anna, my cheeky grandmother Oma Inge, my stern grandfather Opa Martin and my patient fiancée Ronald.

Most importantly I would like to acknowledge my spirit helpers over the other side. I appreciate your generosity, kindness, compassion, strength, love, joy and knowledge to create this beautiful oracle card deck.

Thank you so much for all of your support.

To my adopted father-in-law, who encouraged me to read any book so that I would work on my grammar and English when I was a young child. My challenge was to speak and write clearly without any fear.

Follow your dreams and inspirations, anyone can do it!

A special thank you to Alissa Alpenhof for helping with the beginnings of the first design concept with the oracle cards and ideas for a book cover.

Another lovely lady that stepped into the gallery, Miss Emily Timms who introduced herself as a graphic designer and photographer. Her expertise and efficiency is to be recommended, she actually organised myself to get more motivated to complete this book project.

A gentle push from Spirit to get this on the move!

Many grateful thanks to Miss Shereena Ali, the proof reader for this oracle card deck who has helped with her time and typing to get it all together.

The most important part for acknowledgement is to Ann Wilson, Renée Bahr and Anne-Marie Tripp of Post Pre-press Group for bringing the project together.

I am grateful for this professional assistance to finalise the guide deck book and to get it under way!

A special thank you to Bethaney Brant and Kerrie Alcock from Southport World Wide Print.

Also to Mark Lutz from Art House Reproductions where each painting was professionally photographed, scanned and colour corrected in preparation for giclee reproduction art prints.

My journey into the unknown has been an exciting time in my life, filled with passion, a love for our precious Earth, Mother Nature and to save all creatures great and small!

May you enjoy the art and connecting to colour healing!

P.S Did you know that it is up to the fairies to decide what is the best selection of colours to improvise for every plant, flower, tree, shrub and other plant species that are found on Mother Earth!

Lots of love, light and blessings!
Sylvia 'The Elf'

RECOMMENDED FURTHER READING

Ted Andrews: *How to Heal with Colour*. Llewellyn Publications. 2006.

Lilian Verner-Bonds: *Colour for Healing and Harmony*. Anness Publishing Limited. 1999.

Lillian Verner-Bonds: *Healing with Colour*. Anness Publishing Limited. 2001.

Mike Booth with Carol McKnight: *The Aura-Soma Sourcebook*. Healing Arts Press. 2006.

Irene Dalichow and Mike Booth: *Aura-Soma Healing Through Colour, Plant and Crystal Energy*. Hay House Inc. 1996.

Richard Gerber, M.D.: *Vibrational Medicine*. Bear & Company. 1988.

Julie Gunstone and Pascale Osanz: *Colour Therapy*. Penguin Books – Australia Ltd. 1994.

Faith Jauane and Dusty Bunker: *Numerology and the Divine Triangle*. Whitford Press. 1979.

Louise L. Haye: *You Can Heal Your Life*. Hay House Inc. 1999.

MORE INFORMATION ON THE ARTIST AND ORDER DETAILS FOR ART AND GICLEE REPRODUCTION ART PRINTS

THE COLOUR MEDICINE ORACLE CARD DECK

Sylvia Meissner is an author, illustrator, artist, colour therapist, psychic, medium, intuitive healer and numerologist.

She has worked in her field of practice for over 34 years, managing her own New Age Art Gallery concept stores within Australia. Her mission is to help mankind in the fields of self-help healing through colour therapy, spiritual counselling for guidance, consultant as a master colourist for holistic interiors and businesses, a space clearer and a visionary of ideas and concepts connecting to the laws of divine creation.

The purpose of this oracle guide deck book is to help advance mankind's spiritual evolution towards enlightenment and further unfoldment towards a path of higher consciousness.

The human body is a living network of energy; in fact we are 'Light Beings' who rely upon the sun for survival!

In her own statement, she believes that, 'We can benefit from working and understanding with the laws of colour as a tool for wellness, healing, upliftment, harmony, balance, to enhance health and to promote longevity.'

Her message relates to 'Tapping into Colour Consciousness' through her art, an exhibition that was publicised in The Dubai Times in 2006. Another editorial written by B Magazine called her 'The Rainbow Warrior' with an art event organised in Hong Kong in 1999.

The artist's theory on healing through colour and nature also supports an environmental message for mankind to become more active as being 'The Green-Keeper and the Guardian' for the earth.

We must respect Mother Nature which also includes the animal, mineral and plant kingdoms. The greatest challenge is to learn to share with all other co-habitants on the earth in harmony! Mother Nature, a supernatural power created from the divine source, is warning the planet that it has become out of balance!

The book teaches positive affirmations and meditation techniques through visualisation of colours and illustrates beautiful art works delivered by the artist.

The understanding and advancement of colour light technology will be further used into the 21st century.

To find more information on her creativity of art works please visit:
www.healingartdesign.com.au
Overseas calls: # 61 (0) 408868793
Email address: healingartdesign@outlook.com
or sylviameissner@hotmail.com

You can order on line any of the art reproduction prints on high quality poly-cotton canvas or archival paper (limited sizing) or interested in purchasing any of the original artworks.

Any of the costs for postage, professional packing, shipping and insurance fees will be incurred by the purchaser.

Heal your life with 'Colour' that uplifts your spirit, makes you feel happy, re-energises your body it is like having a dose of light medicine that comes from Mother Nature!

THE MESSAGE FROM HEALING ART DESIGN.

The Sun: represents optimism, happiness and the power of positive thinking!

The Rainbow: allows the window of healing for mankind through colour vibration.

The Heart and Angel Wings: are our guides and soul spirit to know thy self in every way.

The Star: promotes hope, success, protection, wishes fulfilled and divine guidance.

www.ingramcontent.com/pod-product-compliance
Lightning Source LLC
Chambersburg PA
CBHW062033290426
44109CB00026B/2615